JOHN HENRY NEWMAN AND THE ENGLISH SENSIBILITY

T&T Clark Studies in English Theology

Series editors
Karen Kilby
Michael Higton
Stephen R. Holmes

JOHN HENRY NEWMAN AND THE ENGLISH SENSIBILITY

Distant Scene

Jacob Phillips

LONDON • NEW YORK • OXFORD • NEW DELHI • SYDNEY

T&T CLARK
Bloomsbury Publishing Plc
50 Bedford Square, London, WC1B 3DP, UK
1385 Broadway, New York, NY 10018, USA
29 Earlsfort Terrace, Dublin 2, Ireland

BLOOMSBURY, T&T CLARK and the T&T Clark logo are trademarks of
Bloomsbury Publishing Plc

First published in Great Britain 2023
Paperback edition published 2025

Copyright © Jacob Phillips, 2023

Jacob Phillips has asserted his right under the Copyright, Designs and Patents Act, 1988,
to be identified as Author of this work.

Cover image: clairevis/iStock

All rights reserved. No part of this publication may be reproduced or transmitted in
any form or by any means, electronic or mechanical, including photocopying,
recording, or any information storage or retrieval system, without prior permission in
writing from the publishers.

Bloomsbury Publishing Plc does not have any control over, or responsibility for, any
third-party websites referred to or in this book. All internet addresses given in this
book were correct at the time of going to press. The author and publisher regret any
inconvenience caused if addresses have changed or sites have ceased to exist, but can
accept no responsibility for any such changes.

A catalogue record for this book is available from the British Library.

Library of Congress Cataloging-in-Publication Data
Names: Phillips, Jacob, author.
Title: John Henry Newman and the English sensibility : distant scene / by Jacob Phillips.
Description: London ; New York : T&T Clark, 2022. | Series: T&T Clark
studies in English theology | Includes bibliographical references and index. |
Identifiers: LCCN 2022027078 (print) | LCCN 2022027079 (ebook) |
ISBN 9780567689016 (hardback) | ISBN 9780567709998 (paperback) |
ISBN 9780567689023 (pdf) | ISBN 9780567689047 (epub)
Subjects: LCSH: Newman, John Henry, Saint, 1801–1890. | Oxford Movement. |
National characteristics, English–Religious aspects–Anglican Communion. |
National characteristics, English–Religious aspects–Catholic Church. |
Reserve (Christian theology). | Theology–England–History–19th century.
Classification: LCC BX4700.N45 P45 2022 (print) | LCC BX4700.N45 (ebook)
| DDC 282–dc23/eng/20221118
LC record available at https://lccn.loc.gov/2022027078
LC ebook record available at https://lccn.loc.gov/2022027079

ISBN: HB: 978-0-5676-8901-6
PB: 978-0-5677-0999-8
ePDF: 978-0-5676-8902-3
eBook: 978-0-5676-8904-7

Series: T&T Clark Studies in English Theology

Typeset by Newgen KnowledgeWorks Pvt. Ltd., Chennai, India

To find out more about our authors and books visit www.bloomsbury.com
and sign up for our newsletters.

'The death of God for love of us is beyond any culture. It submerges all culture.'
Cardinal Robert Sarah

CONTENTS

Chapter 1
NEWMAN AND ENGLISHNESS — 1
  1.1 The question of Newman's 'Englishness' — 1
  1.2 The trajectory of Englishness in Newman's theology — 5

Chapter 2
THE ENGLISH SENSIBILITY — 13
  2.1 Notions of an English sensibility in Newman's milieu — 13
  2.2 Difficulties with 'Englishness' — 17
  2.3 Three aspects of the English sensibility — 23

Chapter 3
NEWMAN'S TRACTARIAN COMPROMISE — 31
  3.1 Tractarian radical conservatism — 31
  3.2 The radical conservatism of the *Prophetical Office* — 34
  3.3 The tensions of the *Prophetical Office* — 36
  3.4 Summary — 40

Chapter 4
NEWMAN'S TRACTARIAN RESERVE — 41
  4.1 Background to *Arians* — 42
  4.2 Reserve in *Arians* — 44
  4.3 Difficulties with *Arians* — 49
  4.4 Summary — 50

Chapter 5
NEWMAN'S TRACTARIAN EMPIRICISM — 53
  5.1 Action over idea in the *Parochial and Plain Sermons* — 54
  5.2 Common sense pragmatism — 58
  5.3 Summary — 60

Chapter 6
COMPROMISE IN THE SECOND SPRING — 63
  6.1 The event of 1841 — 63
  6.2 Against Englishness — 67
    6.2.1 Against the Englishness of the *via media* — 67
    6.2.2 Against English 'viewiness' — 69
  6.3 Summary — 71

Chapter 7
RESERVE IN THE SECOND SPRING — 73
7.1 Metaphysical developments in ideas in the *Development* essay — 73
7.2 Reserve questioned — 74
    7.2.1 The supernatural virtue of faith in *Difficulties* — 74
    7.2.2 On Marian devotion — 78
    7.2.3 A cultivated intellect in the *Idea of a University* — 78
7.3 Summary — 79

Chapter 8
EMPIRICISM IN THE SECOND SPRING — 83
8.1 The *Development* essay as an empirical inquiry — 83
8.2 Industry in *Difficulties* and the *Present Position* — 87
8.3 Pragmatism and law in *Difficulties* — 88
8.4 Summary — 90

Chapter 9
COMPROMISE IN THE MATURE NEWMAN — 93
9.1 Truth as a virtue and the *Apologia* — 94
    9.1.1 The Kingsley controversy and Englishness — 94
    9.1.2 Truth as a virtue and the *Apologia* — 97
    9.1.3 Anglicanism as a 'halfway house' — 100
9.2 System and mystery in the *Grammar* — 102
9.3 Freeborn subjects of the pope — 104
9.4 Summary — 106

Chapter 10
RESERVE IN THE MATURE NEWMAN — 109
10.1 Affections and passions — 110
    10.1.1 Affections and passions in the *Apologia* — 110
    10.1.2 Affections and passions in the *Grammar* — 111
10.2 Dogmatic formulations as positive in the *Grammar* — 117
10.3 Summary — 118

Chapter 11
EMPIRICISM IN THE MATURE NEWMAN — 121
11.1 The illative sense — 121
11.2 Pragmatic development and empirical consciousness — 126
11.3 Summary — 128

Chapter 12
CONCLUSION: DISTANT SCENE — 129

Bibliography — 133
Index — 137

Chapter 1

NEWMAN AND ENGLISHNESS

1.1 The question of Newman's 'Englishness'

In his celebrated *An Essay on the Development of Christian Doctrine* (1845), St John Henry Newman outlines seven notes of authentic doctrinal developments in Christianity, the third of which he calls 'the power of assimilation'. This is an impulse he considers intrinsic to doctrinal development, whereby Christianity 'grows by taking into its substance external materials'. This 'absorption or assimilation is completed when the materials appropriated come to belong to it and enter into its unity'. Doctrines, he states, 'are not placed in a void, but in the crowded world, and make way for themselves by interpenetration, and develop by absorption'. The assimilation is not presented as unidirectional; it is not that Christianity simply overrides the elements of the world with which it comes into contact and subsumes them. It is rather that such elements expound, extend, and expand the range of doctrine, enabling it to unfold and explicate itself ever more fully and extensively.[1]

Moreover, Newman's description of the assimilative process is not purely eirenic. The process of assimilation requires that external materials are 'subjected to a new sovereign', bringing them under the influence of a 'new element of order and composition'. The 'living idea' of Christianity thus 'becomes many' in taking into itself all manner of things, yet it does so while it 'remains one', maintaining a 'continuity of principle' or 'unity of type', which means genuine assimilation is a form of development which by no means derails the integrity of the faith. On the contrary, doctrinal developments which exhibit this 'power of assimilation' are those which are genuinely authentic; 'life is proved by this capacity of expansion'.[2]

---

1. John Henry Newman, *An Essay on the Development of Christian Doctrine*, edited by James Cameron (Middlesex: Pelican Books, 1974), pp. 130–1. Hereafter: *Development*. Please note the 1845 edition of the *Development* essay is used most often in this book, which tracks the development of Newman's theology and is thus concerned with Newman's position in 1845 rather than when he revised the text for the significantly different 1878 edition. For that revised edition, see John Henry Newman, *An Essay on the Development of Christian Doctrine*, edited by Ian Ker (Indiana: University of Notre Dame Press, 1989), hereafter: *Development 2*.

2. 'Continuity of Principle' is the term used in the 1845 edition, 'Unity of Type' in 1878.

The elements at play which are derived from the 'crowded world' themselves differ in their own readiness and capacity to interpenetrate with Christianity. He maintains that the 'more readily' Christianity 'coalesces' the 'raw material' of its context, the degree to which there is 'an antecedent affinity' between them is indicated.[3] Again, however, Christianity corrects its contexts. He writes, Christianity succeeds by 'purifying' and 'transmuting' as well as 'assimilating' and 'taking into itself the many-colored beliefs, forms of worship, codes of duty, [and] schools of thought, through which it was ever moving'.[4]

Newman's *Development* essay is today often considered 'one of the great theological classics', his 'magnum opus', and a 'masterpiece', and its status is no doubt due in part to the fact he himself accepted the inevitability of his own conversion to Catholicism while working on the book, as a consequence of what he discovered by writing it.[5] The theological literature on the text is of course voluminous, and there is broad consensus as to its importance for Catholic theology right up to the present day.[6] Despite such recognition, however, few have transposed the dynamics of the essay into the circumstances of Newman's own theological work. That is, few have asked how the substance of his own theological positions bears traces of the 'crowded world' of Victorian England. To do so would mean locating contextual elements which perhaps serve as 'antecedent affinities' coalescing with, and absorbed by, Catholicism. Other elements would perhaps be corrected and transmuted as they are 'subjected to a new sovereign'. The question is how exactly Newman witnesses to the encounter between his own cultural context and the Catholicism which became all the more resurgent in the decades following Queen Victoria's coronation, by applying the power of assimilation to Newman's theology itself.

This book seeks to answer this question, and, by doing so, cast light on what it means to consider Newman's theology 'English'. The power of assimilation is an helpful lens for this enquiry, insofar as it offers a way to understand there to be both constructive and destructive elements at work in the encounter between Catholicism and 'Englishness' in Newman's theology, both coalescences and

---

3. Newman, *Development*, p. 187.
4. Ibid., pp. 356-7.
5. Ian Ker in the Introduction to the 1878 edition of *Development*, p. xxv; Thomas G. Guarino, *Vincent of Lérins and the Development of Christian Doctrine* (Grand Rapids, MI: Baker Academic, 2013), pp. 43; Benedict Thomas Viviano, *Catholic Hermeneutics Today: Critical Essays* (Eugene, OR: Wipf and Stock, 2014), p. 131.
6. Ian Ker writes in the introduction to the 1878 edition that Newman remains the 'main inspiration and source' for Catholic theologians writing on doctrinal development to this day. *Development 2*, p. xxv. Gerard H. McCarren, 'The Development of Doctrine', in *The Cambridge Companion to John Henry Newman*, edited by Ian Ker and Terrence Merrigan (Cambridge: Cambridge University Press, 2009), pp. 118-36, writes, 'the compatibility between Newman's Essay and the understanding of doctrinal development espoused by the Second Vatican Council is conspicuous', p. 118.

corrections. After all, asides about Newman as distinctively 'English' are common. These often focus on his prose style, as indeed a fellow Tractarian Hugh Rose commented on his manuscript for *Arians of the Fourth Century* in 1833 as being 'distinctively English'. This view has since been echoed by Anne Fremantle calling Newman 'the most intensely English of English figures',[7] Charles Sarolea's description of him as 'an English classic' who 'gave an infinite picturesqueness to English letters',[8] or Lord Morley calling him one of the 'most winning writers of English that ever existed'.[9]

Some present the substance of Newman's theology itself as proximate to Englishness. Examples here include J. H. Walgrave OP, who claims there is a Platonism at work in Newman which issues 'directly from certain traditional forms of English thought',[10] along with a supposed 'egotism' which he calls 'a very English quality'.[11] Similar tendencies are said by Daniel J. Honan to evince Newman's 'lyrical personality', which is to blame – we read – for 'the shoulder-shrugging of Continental thinkers' when Newman is mentioned.[12] Another example is John Coulsen, who claims that Newman's whole approach to the question of development 'shows to what extent he is within … a common English tradition'.[13] This has recently been echoed by John Cornwell, who says Newman has 'an imaginative apprehension of the Church that is peculiarly English … and alien to scholastic and Roman ways of thinking about development'.[14] Newman is almost unanimously considered centrally important for the development of modern Catholic theology, so there are good grounds to investigate what elements of his 'Englishness' are indeed absorbed and assimilated into his Catholic theology.

At the same time, however, recognitions of Newman's supposed 'Englishness' are often more complex. Going back at least as far as Cardinal Manning's funeral homily in 1890, Newman is presented not as a mere passive reflection of the Englishness proximate to him but as someone who stood apart from his context to a degree sufficient enough to transform it. Manning spoke in wonder about

---

7. Ann Fremantle, 'Newman and English Literature', in *A Newman Symposium*, edited by Victor R. Yanitelli (New York: Fordham University Press, 1952), pp. 143–9, 149.

8. F. A. D'Curz K. S. G., *Cardinal Newman: His Place in Religion and Literature* (Madras: Good Pastor Press, 1935), pp. 1–2.

9. Quoted by Fremantle, 'Newman and English Literature', p. 149.

10. J. H. Walgrave O. P., *Newman the Theologian: The Nature of Belief and Doctrine as Exemplified in His Life and Works* (New York: Sheed & Ward, 1960), pp. 17–18.

11. Ibid., p. 76.

12. Daniel J. Honan, 'Newman's Poetry', in *A Newman Symposium*, edited by Victor R. Yanitelli (New York: Fordham University Press, 1952), pp. 92–6, 94.

13. John Coulsen, *Newman and the Common Tradition: A Study in the Language of Church and Society* (Oxford: Oxford University Press, 1970), p. 55.

14. John Cornwell, *Newman's Unquiet Grave: The Reluctant Saint* (London: Continuum 2010), p. 89.

the fact 'that the public voice of England ... should for once unite in love and veneration' for one who had 'committed the hitherto unpardonable sin in England'. In this way, says Manning, 'the mind of England is changed' by Newman.[15] For, 'the expression of heartfelt English sentiment for a good Roman Catholic would have been impossible a quarter of a century ago'.[16]

Newman is therefore presented not only as proximate to his English context, but in some respects distant from it as well. A recognition of this distance has been linked to Newman's personality, for example, by Edward Short, who considers that Newman 'could not fail to see' the value of 'his own persistent resolve to live the devout life ... for the English people, who had all but lost the sense of what sanctity means'.[17] A motif of distance has even been applied to the Englishness of Newman's prose, by none other than Gerald Manly Hopkins. Hopkins says Newman 'does *not* follow the common tradition' of English writing, he began again 'from the language of ... common life'.[18] A critical distance also applies to interpretations of the theology. One of the clearest examples of this is Weatherby, again, who describes the 1820s and 1830s as a time when the intellectual tradition 'was collapsing in England ... [as Newman's] thought was taking its characteristic shape'. Weatherby sees this tradition climaxing in 'the accomplishments of English theology and poetry' up to the end of the eighteenth century,[19] before Newman heralded 'the death of an order' with his 'departure from the old orthodoxy of England'.[20]

Many would rightly question Weatherby today, but there is an enduring tension between the proximity and distance of Newman to Englishness going right back to his own time. Interestingly, suppositions that Newman is profoundly English and profoundly un-English can coalesce in the same interpretations and even sometimes within the same sentence. Take the aforementioned comment from Anne Fremantle. This reads, 'It is a curious thing, but the most intensely English of English figures, such as Horatio Nelson and John Henry Newman, have almost always been possessed of a capacity for a very un-English expression of emotion'.[21] Such coalescences affect interpretations of the theology. As Coulsen writes on the issue of doctrinal development, 'the way [Newman] sets up the question shows to what extent he is within ... a common English tradition, (but) [his] conclusions

---

15. Quoted by D'Curz, *Cardinal Newman*, p. 479.

16. Ibid.

17. Edward Short, *Newman and His Contemporaries* (London: T&T Clark Continuum, 2011), p. 2.

18. Hopkins says Newman would have seen Gibbon as 'the last great master of English prose', *Further Letters of Gerard Manley Hopkins including His Correspondence with Coventry Patmore*, edited by Claude Colleer Abbott (Oxford: Oxford University Press, 1938), p. 232; cf. Short, *Contemporaries*, pp. 392–3, for a fuller discussion of this.

19. Weatherby, *Cardinal Newman in His Age*, p. 7.

20. Ibid., p. 1.

21. Fremantle, 'Newman and English Literature', p. 149.

... seem at odds with that tradition', for 'parts of the English tradition are to be found re-expressed with an unfamiliar and at times uncongenial setting'.[22] In short, examining such sentiments promises to offer examples of which elements of 'Englishness' necessitate 'correction' and 'transmutation' if they are to assimilate with the Catholic faith.

1.2 The trajectory of Englishness in Newman's theology

Applying the power of assimilation to Newman's 'Englishness' promises to integrate both sides to statements like those above, providing a rationale for unpicking how and why Newman sometimes seems either particularly 'English' or 'un-English'. The first step towards this end is to define what this term 'Englishness' should involve if applied to Newman's life and work, a task undertaken in Chapter 2. There, attention is given to received notions of 'Englishness' in and around the milieu of nineteenth-century England, presenting certain tropes of a supposed Englishness which often endure to this day in contemporary literature. These three tropes resonate with Newman's earliest theological concerns. There is firstly what is termed an 'instinct for compromise', which applies most perceptibly to Newman's work on the Anglican *via media*. There is secondly an 'affection for reserve', which clearly relates to the Tractarian *ethos* Isaac Williams describes as evincing 'quiet resignation'.[23] Thirdly, there is a marked 'empiricism' at play, which is shown by the sheer practicality of the focus on obedience in his *Parochial and Plain Sermons*, not to mention Newman's consistent disdain for things which are 'unreal' or 'paper'.[24]

Moreover, Newman also uses a cluster of terms to point to compromise, reserve, and empiricism as pertaining to what we today would term 'culture', although this word had different meanings in Newman's day.[25] He thus mentions

---

22. Coulsen, *Common Tradition*, p. 55.

23. See particularly Isaac Williams' Tracts 80 and 87 'On Reserve in Communicating Religious Knowledge', and his Tract 87 'Indications of a Superintending Providence in the Preservation of the Prayer Book and in the Changes it has Undergone', where he speaks of the 'peculiar and distinguishing ἦθος in our Church ... [shown by] a quiet resignation and temper of repose', quoted by Cameron in the introduction to *Development*, p. 19.

24. Newman's use of these phrases is so frequent that an exhaustive list would be excessive, but for examples see his sermon on 'Unreal Words' in John Henry Newman, *Parochial and Plain Sermons* (San Francisco, CA: Ignatius Press, 1997), pp. 977–87; comments about the *via media* as 'paper religion' in *Characteristics from the writings of John Henry Newman*, edited by William Samuel Lilly (New York: Scribner, Welford, & Armstrong, 1875), p. 37; and the distinction between 'notional' and 'real' apprehension in John Henry Newman, *An Essay in Aid of a Grammar of Assent* (London: Burns, Oates, 1870) [hereafter: *Grammar*], pp. 34–9.

25. See Jacob Phillips, 'Raymond Williams' Reading of Newman's the Idea of a University', *New Blackfriars*, vol. 102, no. 1097 (2021), and Chapter 2 of this book.

these tendencies as pertaining to things like 'national sentiment', the 'English mind', distinctively English 'characteristics', or 'habits of mind', a 'turn of mind', or a 'genius'.[26] There can be little doubt that Newman understands there to be something along the lines of what Robert Winder has called a 'set of habitual responses' belonging to Englishness, for which Chapter 2 concludes the most appropriate word is 'sensibility'.[27] This clears the way to investigate how this English sensibility interacts with Newman's theology as it develops and transforms throughout his written corpus.

The critical examination commences with Chapters 3–5, examining how Newman's Tractarian works interplay with compromise, reserve, and empiricism, respectively. The mere mention of what came to be called the 'Oxford Movement' calls to mind a quintessential Englishness, of Oxford gentlemen sitting at high table and in quire, or taking dignified constitutionals alongside the Isis to discuss the finer points of obscure patristic controversies. When this superficial supposition is investigated however, a certain un-Englishness to Tractarianism also becomes apparent. That is, while the tendencies of compromise, reserve, and empiricism are undoubtedly perceptible in Tractarian writings, these texts are still often markedly countercultural, and sometimes deliberately provocative. This is particularly true of Newman's contributions, which frequently goad the English avoidance of the extremes of controversy (compromise), for example, not to mention the watering down of Gospel truth in the name of pragmatic and practical settlements in the political sphere (related to empiricism).

Chapter 3's discussion of compromise in Newman's Tractarian writings shows that, in the *Prophetical Office of the Church* (1837), Newman explicitly commends a certain 'indeterminateness' pertaining the *via media* as illustrative of the 'characteristic calmness and caution' of English theology. This arises from the Anglican avoiding of opposed 'solemn anathaemas', because 'virtue lies in a mean'.[28] Yet, the primary purpose of this same work is precisely to determine the specifics of the *via media*. This not only stands in an uneasy tension with Newman's commendation of 'indeterminateness', it is also described by him as necessary to

---

26. Examples: For 'the English mind', see John Henry Newman, *Loss and Gain* (Leominster: Gracewing, 2014), p. 84; for 'characteristics', see John Henry Newman, *Lectures on the Prophetical Office of the Church: Via Media Volume 1* (London: Longmans, Green, 1901), p. 129 [hereafter: *Prophetical Office*]; for 'the English character', see John Henry Newman, *Lectures on the Present Position of Catholics in England* (Leominster: Gracewing, 2000) [hereafter: *Present Position*], p. 57; for 'turn of mind', see *Present Position*, p. 63; for 'genius', see the Postscript to Tract 73; for 'habits of mind', see John Henry Newman, *Apologia pro vita sua* (London: J. M. Dent, 1993), p. 296. (I have used this edition of the Apologia throughout, because it keeps to the original ordering of the first edition, following the letters and pamphlets between Newman and Kingsley chronologically, see Chapter 9.)

27. Robert Winder, *The Last Wolf: The Hidden Springs of Englishness* (London: Little, Brown Group, 2017), pp. 391 and 416–17.

28. Newman, *Prophetical Office*, p. 129.

avoid rendering an ecclesiological motif of creedal Christianity 'mere literature', meaning something merely cultural, a mere expression of the English sensibility rather than revealed truth.[29]

Similar tensions are also found in Chapter 4's examination of reserve in the early Newman, particularly *Arians of the Fourth Century*. This book has discretion and reserve as primary themes, connected even to such integral aspects of Christian thought as allegory and typology, thus putting discretion to use to safeguard the awesome sanctity of mysteries like the Triune God or the transformation of the Eucharistic species. Newman applies reserve to dogmatic formulations, which are presented as a necessary but unfortunate consequence of doctrinal controversy. There are problems here, however. The reserve Newman celebrates in the ancient Alexandrian Church was a mere temporary stage in the path of Christian initiation, and the imparting of the fullness of dogma after full initiation can hardly be understood as something regrettable but necessary. The tension suggests Newman may be guilty of uncritically elevating a tendency of the English sensibility beyond the realm of culture and into theology, to the detriment of the theology itself, in this case, dogma. Again, there is the threat of making Christian faith reducible to 'mere literature'.

Chapter 5 turns to empiricism in the Tractarian period, focusing on a pronounced prioritizing of 'action over ideas' in Christian obedience seen particularly in the *Parochial and Plain Sermons*. At the same time, however, this chapter gives attention to Newman's willingness to deviate from the traditional principles of empiricism as pragmatism in his discussions of the *via media* in the *Prophetical Office* and the *Tracts for the Times*. In both examples, Newman criticizes those unimaginative and timid contemporaries of his who seek to protect the status quo from the fiery zeal of the Tractarians. We are thus faced again with an uneasy tension, for Newman seems to make the empirical world the centre of gravity for the entirety of the Christian life in his sermons, yet at the same time he wants to tackle the centrality of the empirical world for Anglican ecclesiology. When it comes to empiricism, then, Newman seems both to extend or intensify empiricism on one front, while questioning and challenging it on another.

The importance of Newman's 1845 conversion to Catholicism for understanding his life can hardly be overstated, and the importance of this event for his theology is of course similarly immense. This middle period of Newman's life is of particular importance for this book for three reasons. Firstly, it is where, having now articulated the idea of the power of assimilation in the *Development* essay, Newman himself applies this to his own context, albeit negatively. In his *Difficulties of Anglicans* from 1850, he uses the principles enunciated in the *Development* essay to convince his former co-religionists that their purportedly 'catholic' convictions could never be assimilated and absorbed by the Anglican Church, because the fundamental 'principles' or 'type' of that church is intrinsically antithetical to Catholicism. The Anglican formularies are 'but the expression of national sentiment', he claims, and

29. Ibid., p. 22.

so cannot assimilate Tractarian commitments: just as 'physical life assimilates to itself, or casts off, whatever it encounters' and allows 'no interference with the supremacy of its own proper principles'.[30] For Anglicanism, all is subject to the 'sovereign Lord and Master of the Prayer-Book' and 'its composer and interpreter' who is just 'the Nation itself', and not God.[31]

Secondly, this middle period is important as the juncture where Newman sees his own English context from the outside.[32] It is nearly always the case that proximity to people of different contexts to one's own enables one to see one's own context afresh, and this is intensified in Newman's case because Catholicism had begun to revisit the perpetual challenge of situating particulars, like cultural identity, in relation to its universal provenance. In *Difficulties*, Newman quotes in full the following paragraph from the 1843 translation of Johann Adam Möhler's *Symbolik*:

> Each nation is endowed with a peculiar character, stamped on the deepest, most hidden parts of its being, which distinguishes it from all other nations, and manifests its peculiarity in public and domestic life, in art and science; in short, in every relation. In every general act of a people, the national spirit is infallibly expressed; and should contests ... occur, the element destructive to the vital principle of the whole will most certainly be detached in them.[33]

This not only offers a focused expression of the notion of national sensibilities in Newman's work, it mirrors almost exactly the biological and organic notion of growth through rejection or acceptance of developments in line with a 'vital principle' from the *Development* essay. This leads to the third reason why this middle period is highly important for this book. Newman's 1852 sermon 'The Second Spring' is infamous as a clarion call for the revival of Catholicism in England that followed the restoration of the hierarchy in 1850, coming shortly after the wave of conversions that followed Newman to Rome.[34] While the sermon is hugely well known, however, few commentators draw attention to the substance of its argument.

'The Second Spring' is presented not simply as a religious revival of the Old Faith, but rather as something that goes directly against the development of

---

30. John Henry Newman, *Certain Difficulties Felt by of Anglicans in Catholic Teaching Volume 1* (New York: Longmans, Green, 1901), p. 19.

31. Ibid., pp. 14–15.

32. See Ian Ker, *John Henry Newman* (Oxford: Oxford University Press, 2010), pp. 316–36.

33. Quoted by Newman, in *Difficulties*, p. 54.

34. See Ker, *Newman*, pp. 381–2: 'Most of the bishops and clergy were in tears, including Wiseman.' It is worth noting that Joseph C. Keenan estimates around 4,000 people 'followed Newman' to Rome, Joseph C. Keenan, 'Newman's Significance', in *A Newman Symposium*, pp. 135–9, 136.

national life according to an approach like Möhler's, and indeed Newman's own *Development* principles. That is, this sermon portrays the rebirth of Catholicism in England as a radical break, breach, or rupture with the developing trajectory of England itself. He says that the 'noblest efforts' of human 'genius', including 'the conquests he has made, the doctrines he has originated, the nations he has civilized, the states he has created' will inevitably end in 'dissolution'. However, 'in England', he continues, 'something strange is passing over this land, for something which was dissolved is miraculously coming back to life'. This is miraculous, he says, for it is 'a restoration in the moral world' like that of the 'physical world', and such has never been seen before, like 'the coming in of a Second Spring'. In other words, 'grace can, where nature cannot'.[35]

The notion of a miraculous breach from England's dissolution serves for this book as emblematic of this middle period in Newman's work, from around the time of the conversion to around the time of the *Apologia pro vita sua* of 1864. During these years, the English sensibility is discarded as Newman comes under the influence of the new 'sovereign': Catholicism. The subtextual tensions around Englishness in the Tractarian writings undergo a marked transformation, insofar as those countercultural elements of that earlier period are now intensified to the degree that Newman mounts a full-scale assault on the English sensibility itself. As Frank M. Turner has it, 'the Tractarian pursuit of the Catholic led as much to *cultural* as to *religious* apostasy'.[36]

The specifics of this proceed as follows. Chapter 6 brings the most marked 'break' in Newman's thinking into view, focusing on compromise, as the *via media*, which he of course recants through the *Development* essay, marking what he considers the most transformative moment of his thought.[37] His assaults on Englishness flourish most vehemently in his satires, where he unleashes the full force of his prose against some of the corollaries of celebrating compromise: a fondness for free thinking, or the 'free born Englishman' who can choose between extremes without the threat of anathemas, not to mention opting for expedience, or concord, to tame religious convictions.

This repudiation applies in some ways to reserve during this Second Spring period as well, as shown in Chapter 7. Strikingly, given reserve's centrality for the earlier *Arians*, Newman aims at it directly by praising the Catholic 'profaneness' of devotion as indicative of a great spiritual benefit long since lost to the English: a simplicity of faith.[38] Yet, a tension comes to light here. While Newman now considers it generally positive that Catholics speak of 'the sacred heart' or the 'mother of mercies', he still maintains his earlier reserve towards dogmatic formulations in his

---

35. John Henry Newman, *Sermons Preached on Various Occasions* (London: Longmans, Green, 1908), pp. 166-7.

36. Frank M. Turner, *John Henry Newman: The Challenge to Evangelical Religion* (Yale: Yale University Press, 2002), p. 294.

37. See Newman, *Difficulties*, pp. 372-3, and Newman, *Apologia*, pp. 155-99.

38. Newman, *Difficulties*, pp. 273-4.

more formal texts. In the *Development* essay, for example, he claims dogmas 'are necessary only because the human mind cannot reflect' on things like the Divine Nature, and so they are only ever 'expressions' of the divine and 'never equivalent to it'.[39] However, it seems inconsistent to consider dogmas to be regrettably limited in their ability to portray the divine, while celebrating how popular devotionalism uncritically and profanely 'chatters away' with other portrayals of divinity. After all, with the Nicene Creed, for example, both elements come together insofar as the dogma is central for both liturgy and theological study.

Chapter 8 turns to empiricism during Newman's middle period, and here again we see Newman going full-throttle against Englishness. The targets are popular understandings of an empirical sensibility expressed by the industrial revolution and the pragmatism of the legal, parliamentarian tradition. Here Newman ferociously argues that English self-confidence usurps the place of God with the self-satisfaction of a highly accomplished cultural identity. But, again, there is a tension. Newman's criticisms of the English sensibility in *Lectures on the Present Position of Catholics in England* include the claim that there is an English antipathy to fact, particularly historical fact, along with the well-documented English hostility to logic. This presents a difficulty, insofar as the essay which led to his own conversion, *Development*, seems itself to use history against logic. Newman's method in this text commonly contrasted with the then-dominant explicatory logic of development in Roman scholasticism. Moreover, in *The Idea of a University* (1858) he maintains that theology has one 'intelligible method', for 'deduction *only*' is its 'sole instrument'.[40] As it stands, Newman's criticisms of Englishness threaten to downplay or even contradict the very book which led to his conversion.

The final period of Newman's writing is discussed in Chapters 9–11, covering the period from the *Apologia* to his death in 1890. This period is described in this book as Newman's 'mature' period, pointing to how he integrates and balances both English and un-English elements of his thinking, particularly in the *Apologia* and the *Essay in Aid of a Grammar of Assent* (1870). The process of writing the *Apologia* seems pivotal here, not just because he charts the development of his intellectual and spiritual development from early childhood onwards but also because his battles with Charles Kingsley meant he had a vested interest in presenting his development as relatively unified and continuous.[41] The *Grammar*, while perhaps the most technical and least personal of Newman's works, is known to be the fruit of a decades-long gestation and aims to be an exhaustive study of its subject matter.

Chapter 9 discerns, nonetheless, that when it comes to the English instinct for compromise, there is no softening of Newman's earlier critique. The reasons

---

39. Newman, *Development*, pp. 114–16.

40. John Henry Newman, *The Idea of a University* (Yale: Yale University Press, 1996), pp. 55 and 154 (my italics) – hereafter: *Idea*.

41. See Chapter 9 for a full discussion of this controversy.

are rooted in his conversion, of course, but it is important to outline exactly how Newman's more conciliatory tone towards Anglicanism in the *Apologia* does not downplay the recanting of ecclesial compromise which led him to Rome. Chapter 10, by contrast, finds there is an important shift on reserve, notwithstanding his dismissals from the previous decade in *Difficulties*. Here, Newman alludes to how a virtue like reserve can be renovated, insofar as it leads *from* faith and does not usurp it. This enables him to acknowledge that dogmas are a cause for celebration and praise, not least liturgically. Chapter 11 finds a final important shift with empiricism. Here, an aspect of the English sensibility receives significant commendation, and little in the way of correction. Indeed, empiricism even shows itself to be intrinsically close to Catholic faith in and of itself. Thus it can be included among what Newman calls 'our own habits of mind' which are able to find 'a place and thereby a sanctification, in the Catholic Church'.[42]

Before undertaking this investigation in the following chapter, two brief disclaimers are necessary. In the first place, it is a weakness of this book that I have stayed sharply focused mostly on Newman's published texts, with little in the way of historical and biographical embellishment of the world going on around those texts, let alone other textual discussions among Newman and his contemporaries. My reasoning is that there is a paucity of secondary scholarship on Newman's Englishness as it pertains to the substance of his theology itself, so this is the book's primary focus.[43] While acknowledgements of Newman being peculiarly English or un-Englishness are common, they are usually passing remarks, and nearly always refer to history, biography, or cultural context alone, rather than detailed elements of his thinking.

Secondly, I have opted throughout this book to avoid, as far as possible, using terminology of 'Roman Catholics' or 'Roman Catholicism'. While such usage is common in secondary literature about Newman, I want to take heed of Newman's own criticisms of this terminology as undermining the meaning of catholicity itself, and as an English anomaly with little or no meaning elsewhere. This reasoning is

---

42. Newman, *Apologia*, p. 296.

43. There are three texts which thematize elements of the relationship between Newman and English thought in Newman's theology, which I have discussed in 'John Henry Newman and the English Sensibility', *Logos*, vol. 24, no. 3 (Summer 2021): 108–29. Firstly, Harold L. Weatherby, *Cardinal Newman in His Age* (Vanderbilt: Vanderbilt University Press, 1973), but Weatherby's argument that Newman 'departs' from the English tradition is not so much focused on the Englishness per se but rather the premodern characteristics of English theology and poetry he feels Newman surrendered to modern impulses. Secondly, Coulsen, *Newman and the Common Tradition*, but this downplays Newman's counter-cultural elements, and neglects the importance of his conversion and the satires. Thirdly is J. H. Walgrave O. P., *Newman the Theologian: The Nature of Belief and Doctrine as Exemplified in His Life and Works* (New York: Sheed & Ward, 1960), but this interprets Newman's introspective qualities as rooted in English Platonism, of which there is little or no trace in the theology itself (see the discussion of Newman and British Empiricism in Chapter 2).

simply faithfulness to authorial intention – to Newman's own position – and not intended as any triumphalism or provocation to the many Anglicans who greatly appreciate Newman's life and work. The same impulse grounds my decision to keep to the strange editorial anomalies of the original *Tracts for the Times*, particularly that Tractarian tendency to capitalize key words and subclauses for impact.

There are of course a litany of disclaimers required for daring to write about a supposed English sensibility at any time, not to mention Newman's lifetime, and indeed my own. For Newman's time, Britain was approaching the high-water mark of Empire, and for my own, English nationhood, ethnicity, and identity are perhaps more fraught with controversy than ever before, at least in the Academy. These issues will be a focus of the following chapter, where the precise meaning of the phrase 'the English sensibility' as it applies to this book will be established, along with discussion of the various limits and nuances which will attend to its use in the chapters to follow.

Chapter 2

THE ENGLISH SENSIBILITY

To speak of an 'English sensibility' presents a multitude of difficulties for both the words involved: 'English' and 'sensibility'. This chapter establishes firstly that notions of different people and places evincing particular characteristics were particularly current in Newman's day, and indeed shared by Newman himself. Moreover, while these notions include superficial differences, they also point to a pervasive moral and aesthetic dimension for which the term 'sensibility' seems particularly apposite to describe. Secondly, this chapter focuses on certain difficulties with writing about national sensibilities, and particularly Englishness, when it comes to questions of Britishness and the fallibility of official narratives, not to mention those questions of ethnicity which have the spectre of British imperialism looming in the background. Thirdly, some of the content of the received notion of an English sensibility is discussed, highlighting those aspects which will prove important for Newman's theology in the chapters to follow.

2.1 Notions of an English sensibility in Newman's milieu

The word 'Englishness' first entered the Oxford Dictionary in 1805, some four years after Newman's birth. It seems strange, at first glance, that a country identified as centuries old should suddenly have coined a substantive to capture what Paul Langford calls a 'summarising [of] the essence' of its nationality in 1805. Langford points out that a Germanophile, William Taylor of Norwich, coined the term, and he suggests the word has a 'Germanic feel' in its mirroring of the equivalent substantive *Deutschtums*.[1] This observation relates to that common phenomenon mentioned in the previous chapter: encounters with unfamiliar cultures often reveal hitherto unnoticed things about one's own culture. Taylor's encounters with the German language may have revealed the lack of a substantive term like *Deutschtums* in his own tongue. Yet in the late eighteenth century the profile of both England and the English was growing on the continent, and there was therefore a corresponding growth in understandings, both at home and abroad, of what an

---

1. Paul Langford, *Englishness Identified: Manners and Character 1650–1850* (Oxford: Oxford University Press, 2001), pp. 1–2.

English 'national character' was thought to involve. Langford writes of 'a growing penetration of English letters on the Continent' which had a 'marked effect' by the 1770s, as indeed the term 'national character' was becoming fashionable.[2]

Against this background, responses to the French Revolution prove definitive in codifying elements of 'Englishness' in the early nineteenth century. Of primary importance here is Edmund Burke, who provides one of the fullest descriptions of national or group character which remained authoritative for many decades.[3] Burke wrote of each 'people' having a certain 'genius', 'temper', or 'manners'.[4] Burke's use of 'manners' is different to the contemporary usage as referring to established norms which are today generally considered more or less arbitrarily different among diverse cultures. For Burke, 'manners' has a much richer semantic field. He writes, 'manners are what vex and sooth, corrupt or purify, exalt or debase, barbarise or refine us, by a constant, steady, uniform, insensible operation, like that of the air we breathe'. Burke concludes that manners 'give the whole form and colour to our lives'.[5]

There is therefore much more at stake in this term 'manners' than just accepted niceties around things like greeting and eating. In the eighteenth century, 'what was called manners' had a 'wider extent and a more fruitful ambiguity' than today.[6] When Burke writes that manners 'corrupt or purify, exalt or debase, barbarise or refine us' it is clear the word is closely linked to what would today be called ethics, and this link is itself particularly perceptive bearing in mind the root term of ethics, ἦθος, can be translated as habit, manner, custom, or morals, although 'ethics' usually means just morality in contemporary English. As Terry Eagleton writes, Burke's manners are not so much a matter of 'social graces' as 'the time-honoured customs and convictions by which men and women live', in an 'intricate mesh of affinities and observances'.[7]

What Eagleton calls 'affinities', and Burke calls a 'constant ... insensible operation' like 'the air we breathe', leads to another way in which 'manners' go far deeper than dos and don'ts. We are dealing here with an unreflective and unarticulated intuitive sense of a good way of living. For Burke, this unreflective dimension of the 'manners' of groups of people functions as the source or origin of distinctive behaviours and patterns of social organization. Anthony Easthope has provided a more modern metaphor for this, by comparing 'national identity' to

---

2. Ibid., pp. 6–7.

3. See David Bromwich, *The Intellectual Life of Edmund Burke: From the Sublime and Beautiful to American Independence* (Cambridge, MA: Belknap Press of Harvard University Press, 2014).

4. Quoted by Conor Cruise O'Brien, *The Great Melody* (London: Sinclair Stevenson, 1992), p. 311.

5. Edmund Burke, *The Portable Burke*, edited by Isaac Kramnik (Harmondsworth: Penguin, 1999), p. 520.

6. Langford, *Englishness*, p. 8.

7. Terry Eagleton, *Culture* (Yale: Yale University Press, 2018), p. 70.

driving a car – a 'pre-conscious integration of perception and movement' in which driving becomes 'an almost spontaneous extension of my bodily self – I inhabit it, I live it'. Easthope's point is that national identity functions as 'an unconscious structure' that 'can speak [for] us even when we may think we are speaking for ourselves', something that 'works at a deeper strata than simply the *content* of the various overtly national practices, narratives, discourses, symbols and tropes through which [it] is conventionally presented'.[8]

The importance of this term 'manners' for speaking of the English sensibility in Newman's day reflects more than the fact Burke was an influential figure in early nineteenth-century England. The increased codification of the English sensibility at this time was due in part to the inheritance and adoption of Burke-esque 'manners' by increasing numbers of the urban middle class. Eagleton states that early eighteenth-century writers such as Joseph Addison, Richard Steele, and Anthony Ashley Cooper use the term 'politeness' for what some would later call culture: 'as a form of graceful conduct which promotes social harmony' and 'unites the moral and aesthetic'. The closeness of such 'politeness' to 'traditional aristocratic values' like 'gentility, affability, elegance, refinement, and the like' made the concept highly attractive to 'an emergent middle class in some need of a spot of polish'. Thus, for Eagleton, adopting a mutual sensibility meant 'the two social classes would be wedded together'.[9] This is worthy of note not least because Newman himself belonged to a later generation of the same emergent, urban middle class, being the son of a banker.[10] The word 'sensibility' seems particularly apposite for capturing the meanings of this refined 'genius', 'temper', or 'manners', insofar as in the late eighteenth century 'sensibility' was closely linked both to polite niceties and the more subtle and amorphous ethical dimension undergirding those niceties.

The word 'culture' is perhaps the most obvious contender for a contemporary alternative to Burke's manners. Raymond Williams famously arrives at the definition of culture as 'a whole way of life' in his seminal work *Culture and Society: 1780–1950*, and this 'whole way of life' approach does indeed correlate loosely with the all-pervasive nature of Burke's 'air' metaphor.[11] However, Williams's analysis charts a complex progression in the meanings of the word 'culture'. He begins by claiming that 'in the last decades of the 18th Century, and in the first half of the 19th, a number of words, which are now of capital importance, came for the first time into common English use, or, … acquired new and important meanings'.[12] Culture is,

---

8. Anthony Easthope, *Englishness and National Culture* (London: Routledge, 1999), pp. 3–5.

9. Eagleton, *Culture*, p. 116; cf. Terry Eagleton, *Literary Theory: An Introduction*, 2nd edn (Oxford: Blackwell, 1996), p. 15.

10. See Ker, *John Henry Newman*, p. 1.

11. Raymond Williams, *Culture and Society 1780–1950* (Harmondsworth: Penguin Books, 1963), p. 18. See Phillips, 'Raymond Williams'.

12. Williams, *Culture and Society*, p. 13.

unsurprisingly, the paradigmatic keyword in this. By means of a careful semantic analysis of its use, Williams tracks 'a general pattern of change' in meaning, which 'can be used as a special kind of map'. He considers 'the questions ... concentrated in the meanings of the word *culture*' to be 'questions directly raised by ... great historical changes',[13] namely industrialization and the widespread social upheaval it brought with it from around 1780 onwards.

Williams's analysis is lengthy and complex, and can only be touched upon here. The main point is that he argues that the word 'culture' began to be used in ways recognizable today relatively late, particularly by Matthew Arnold (1822–88). Williams works from Burke's oft-repeated statement that 'the stock' of reason 'in each man is small, and ... individuals would do better to avail themselves of the general bank and capital of nations and ages'.[14] Wisdom might be a better word to give voice for what Burke includes in the concept of reason; he is pointing to an intergenerational reserve of wisdom which, says Williams, was 'immediately' after Burke called the 'spirit of the nation', and by the end of the nineteenth century came to be known as 'national culture'.[15] But note the important point: the word 'culture' is not at Burke's disposal in the late eighteenth century, and nor, says Williams, was it at Newman's disposal.[16] Therefore, while it is salient that the cluster of terms that Burke (and Newman) use for what Williams claims eventually came to be called 'national culture' align comfortably with much later definitions of culture as 'a whole way of life', the word 'culture' itself has a developing trajectory of different meanings, many of which fail to capture the ethical and unreflective character of those terms like 'manners', 'genius', or 'temper', and so on.

Before approaching certain difficulties with Englishness specifically, suffice to say that there is plentiful evidence that Newman himself broadly shares Burke's contention that there is such a thing as national or group character, or rather national or group 'genius', 'temper', or 'manners'.[17] Of course, his assumptions are only strengthened by his thoroughgoing encounters with foreign people and places through his conversion. These ideas are seen in characters in the novel *Loss and Gain* frequently referring to 'national character', for example, and claiming there is a 'robust, masculine, noble independence in the English mind'.[18] There is

---

13. Ibid.
14. Burke quoted in Williams, *Culture and Society*, p. 28.
15. Williams, *Culture and Society*, p. 30.
16. Cf. Phillips, 'Raymond Williams'. Culture was coming to be understood as referring to a state of *intellectual* cultivation, and Newman thus appears in *Culture and Society* somewhere between culture as related to 'the idea of human perfection', and its morphing into referring to 'the general state of intellectual development, in a society as a whole'. Williams, *Culture and Society*, p. 18.
17. See note 4 above.
18. Newman, *Loss and Gain*, pp. 84–5; for 'national mind' see Newman, *Difficulties*, p. 284.

also Newman's aforementioned discussion of Möhler's writing on each nation's 'peculiar character, stamped on the deepest, most hidden parts of its being, which distinguishes it from all other nations'.[19] We shall see that Newman strongly disagreed that the English mind is robust, masculine, and noble later on, but the point is that such claims were obviously common at this time.[20] Hence, his biting comments about Catholicism appealing to childlike impulses unbefitting of an 'English gentleman',[21] or his writing about the English people as being 'notorious' for taking 'little interest' in 'foreign countries'.[22] The point is that he assumes there are 'peculiarities of the English character', and that the English have a 'natural turn of mind'.[23] This assumption endures in his latest writings. In the *Essay in Aid of a Grammar of Assent*, for example, he discusses at length 'the prejudice which exists against logic in the popular mind' of 'Englishmen'.[24]

Such examples show there are good grounds to investigate Newman's theological writings with a view to scrutinizing the degree to which the notion of an English 'national character' has some influence on his findings. It is also clear that this character includes what Langford describes as 'those distinctive aspects of national life that strike either outsiders or insiders or both as characteristic'.[25] Moreover, insofar as this character explains various instincts, tendencies, presumptions, and dispositions, it also includes a pervasive and unreflective sense for particular 'affinities' seen as undergirding 'social existence as a whole'.[26] That such ideas are understood at best as mere arbitrary quirks today, or at worst as 'repugnant to the liberal conscience of the West',[27] should not blind us to the fact neither of these repudiations apply to Newman himself. It is therefore necessary to look closer at why this is so troublesome to contemporary ears.

2.2 Difficulties with 'Englishness'

One of the first difficulties which must be tackled in speaking of an English sensibility is why I am using the word 'English' rather than 'British'. This difficulty goes right back to the late eighteenth- and early nineteenth-century literature. David Simpson, for example, adopts 'British' in his discussion of British Romanticism, except when speaking of literature as English literature, because

---

19. Newman, *Difficulties*, p. 54.
20. See Chapters 6–8, where Newman's criticisms are discussed at length.
21. Newman, *Difficulties*, p. 229.
22. Newman, *Present Position*, p. 58.
23. Ibid., pp. 57–8, 62; he speaks of 'the character of [our] countrymen' on p. 85.
24. Newman, *Grammar*, pp. 295–6.
25. Langford, *Englishness*, p. 2.
26. Eagleton, *Culture*, p. 115.
27. Langford, *Englishness*, p. 7.

'English' was 'the preferred term' in the early nineteenth century, not British.[28] While Simpson chooses to speak of 'British national character', Stefan Collini in *English Pasts* defends his use of 'English' precisely on the same grounds as Simpson's concession: that 'it was the established usage during much of the period' he is 'concerned with'.[29] Robert Winder has similarly defended his concern with English identity, specifically, but his medieval focus means 'Britain did not exist'.[30] While such cannot be said of Newman's lifetime, Collini's line of defence certainly applies to the nineteenth century as time when the national identity of England was more often spoken of as 'English' rather than 'British'. There are numerous reasons as to why this is the case, not least that the term links directly to the English language in a way that cannot apply now that it is widely spoken across the globe. Perhaps this is why a contemporary of Newman's, Thomas Carlyle – hardly an Englishman by any reckoning – himself refers to his work and mission as 'English' throughout his life.[31]

This book adopts Collini's reasoning on this point, and I would also highlight his observation that 'the entities involved in the frequent comparisons with France and French culture have most often been "England" and "the English"'. He is also right about the importance of underscoring 'the intimacy of the connection with "English literature" which has ... played such a large part in shaping the identity of English culture'.[32] On this last point, it is also worth mentioning Langford's claim that 'it was the sensibility of the English novel' that most defined Englishness in the run-up to the nineteenth century, and that this 'single most potent agent of English culture' was 'par excellence about character and manners'.[33] Langford also offers another reason why using 'Britishness' is not ideal. He observes that characteristics deemed 'British' invariably coincide with allegedly English characteristics, for any characteristic which might be deemed typical of 'the so-called Celtic nations' is distinctive to one or more of those nations, and thus not usually included in 'Britishness'. This means, says Langford, that using 'British' in the name of what we would today call inclusivity 'is indeed precisely to patronise' the other nations 'as the English have often been accused of doing'.[34] While this book adopts 'English' and 'Englishness' on the basis of both Collini and Langford's reasoning, it shares Collini's disclaimer that 'no usage here can be entirely consistent and satisfying'.[35]

28. David Simpson, 'Romanticism, Criticism and Theory', in *The Cambridge Companion to British Romanticism*, edited by Stuart Curran (Cambridge: Cambridge University Press, 1993), pp. 1–24, 3.

29. Stefan Collini, *English Pasts: Essays in History and Culture* (Oxford: Oxford University Press, 1999), p. 4. The period under discussion is the early to mid-twentieth century, but the reasoning applies to Simpson's period too.

30. Winder, *The Last Wolf*, p. 7.

31. John Morrow, *Thomas Carlyle* (London: Continuum, 2006), p. 110.

32. Collini, *English Pasts*, p. 4.

33. Langford, *Englishness*, p. 11.

34. Ibid., p. 14.

35. Collini, *English Pasts*, p. 4.

A second difficulty with speaking of an English sensibility arises from concerns rooted in variants of social theory, and surrounds the question of whether one can rightly speak of there being a specific constellation of attributes and affinities belonging to an English sensibility in the singular without reduction. Collini is particularly critical of singularity here, speaking of 'coercive fictions like "the English tradition"', suggesting a received notion of Englishness is something used by those in authority for manipulation and control.[36] Collini's concern is shared also by Brian Doyle, for whom the Englishness of English Literature is not 'natural but contingent', and based 'on the considerable effort of cultural institution making'.[37] However, both Collini and Doyle focus these arguments on the later nineteenth and early twentieth centuries, a particularly important time during which, as Doyle shows, English literature was growing in popularity over the tradition of Classics within the academy. By Doyle's analysis, the Englishness of literary studies served as a means 'to sustain the notion of a "liberal education" with attendant notions of an aristocratic cultural mystique'. The move from Classics to English literature also gave 'a powerful national dimension' to a liberal education which could even be construed as 'giving English authors a transnational provenance like that traditionally associated with Ovid or Virgil'.[38] By the time the Board of Education commissioned the Newbolt Report in 1921, English literature was thus 'the central pedagogic instrument' in a 'strategy for national cultural renewal'.[39]

Such analyses are helpful in avoiding lazy recourses to an English sensibility as something unproblematically and easily utilized. They show there is often a vast difference between received notions or official histories, and actual reality. It is also crucially important always to remember that any notion of national identity is to some extent reductive, especially when applied to a time where travel and communications meant regional differences were far more pronounced than they are today. However, there are good grounds to suggest that Collini's defence against speaking of 'Britishness' can – during the earlier period during which Newman lived – also be applied to the question of multiple sensibilities: 'it was the established usage' at this time. That is, Newman generally assumes there is an English sensibility in the singular, but from here on it is important to keep in mind that we are dealing with a *received* notion of the English sensibility, with common norms of English self-understanding.

To speak in this way is to focus on the literary classes. This focus does not include the question of how accurate this received notion is, with questions like whether the English were themselves *genuinely* given to compromise and reserve, or just as likely to be as fanatical and crassly outspoken as anyone else. That elements of this received notion were manipulated or exaggerated seems highly likely, and there are of course various examples of purportedly 'un-English' sentiments on

36. Ibid., p. 5.
37. Brian Doyle, *English and Englishness* (London: Taylor and Francis, 2013), p. 1.
38. Doyle, *English*, p. 27; the connections with Empire seem relatively self-evident.
39. Ibid., p. 41.

display in many historical events of the time. An obvious issue related to this is the question of how English writers liked to think of themselves, and the reality of how English and British national identity in the eighteenth and nineteenth centuries was developing in tandem with imperialism. I am not suggesting that English decorum was displayed in barbaric moments of foreign conquest, simply that the English themselves understood their national character to involve that decorum, however misguided their supposition may have been.

It is also important to state that the boundaries of any national sensibility are nearly always relatively porous, that such a sensibility is impossible to delineate exhaustively, and it usually bears multiple variations and exceptions among those who share that identity. To speak of an English sensibility should not be taken as denying multiple regional identities, social class distinctions, and a fair amount of wishful thinking if not overt denial as well. Rather, I am drawing attention to the fact that, across Europe, 'there exists a long tradition of national characterisations, informing every kind of discourse', and that characterizations of Englishness gained currency in the late eighteenth and early nineteenth centuries.[40] These characterizations are not determinate of those to whom they are applied, for 'there are continuities and patterns … which have given intellectual life in England a certain distinctness', and these should be thought of more in terms of relatively fluid 'constellations' than fixed and determinate ideas.[41] Most importantly, a clear sense of particular elements of Englishness is clearly discernible in Newman's life and milieu. Here we encounter another reason why the word 'sensibility' seems particularly apposite. The word is, like 'genius', 'temper', or 'manners', a relatively fluid or porous term, pointing more to a 'disposition' or 'orientation', of tendencies of patterned responses, than anything capable of exhaustively adumbrated and sharply bounded contents.

This leaves a final difficulty which is perhaps the most controversial: race or ethnicity. Insofar as particular characteristics pertaining to a sensibility are thought to be rooted in racial identity, we are dealing here with something described by Paul Langford as 'repugnant to the liberal conscience of the West'.[42] Langford's response to this is to suggest the time period he is concerned with predates the 'explanatory model' of nineteenth- and twentieth-century ideas of race.[43] He also claims that it was not until the mid-nineteenth century that it 'becomes possible to believe the English were racially pure', citing Ruskin's notorious comment that the English were 'undegenerate in race' from 1884.[44] In the eighteenth century particularly, says Langford, there was 'a mongrel principle' applied to English identity as something comprised of different racial identities, quoting Thomas Fielding's comment that 'we are a mixed race, and our character partakes of the

---

40. Langford, *Englishness*, p. 7.
41. Collini, *English Pasts*, p. 1.
42. Langford, *Englishness*, p. 7.
43. Ibid.
44. Ibid., p. 16.

compound nature of our descent' which consist 'not in one predominant quality, but in the union of several'.⁴⁵ This 'mongrel' principle has been revisited more recently by Peter Ackroyd, whose *Albion: The Origins of the English Imagination* extends the principle beyond ethnicity into what he himself terms a 'sensibility'. Ackroyd thus argues that Englishness involves 'a willingness to adapt and adopt other influences', the English character is for him by definition a mongrel character. Similarly Robert Winder argues that 'national character was not a matter of blood' but the 'hybrid product of many identities'.⁴⁶

Ackroyd's discussion of Englishness has a distinctive theme related to the ambiguities of English ethnicities, namely his focus on the definitiveness of the 'land' upon which people in England live. He is a long way from Langford's description of national identities as 'an attempt to describe those differences between people' organized by 'a transitory expression of territorial units', insofar as territory is not for Ackroyd 'transitory' as such. Rather, his focus on the English as people inhabiting a place brings a new dimension to this discussion.⁴⁷ Indeed, this dimension has some precursors, particularly in Nicolaus Pevsner, for whom environment is definitive over national culture, particularly climate.⁴⁸ Ackroyd's basic contention is not entirely dissimilar to Roger Scruton's suggestion that English 'patriotism', like the 'patriotism of the Romans', derives from the fact that 'homeland, rather than race, was the focus of loyalty'.⁴⁹ Part of the reasoning behind an emphasis on place against race is that most of England's borders are coastlines, so the old idea of an 'island nation' is definitive here.

At first glance, a focus on place is highly attractive for my purposes in this book, given the difficulties surrounding race. There are, however, certain points to be made about the limits to speaking of the 'sensibility of England' rather than the 'English sensibility' for these reasons. Firstly, it is necessary to be careful about anachronistically transposing eighteenth-century notions of European races into twenty-first-century contexts. Fielding et al. were talking about ethnicities like Saxon, Celt, Pict, Viking, or Dane, which would by twenty-first-century reckonings all be viewed as pertaining to the same race due to today's dominant association of race and ethnicity with skin colour. This means that, however seductive to today's 'liberal conscience of the West', comments about the English as a 'mongrel people' do not simply sidestep and avoid questions pertaining to English attitudes to people of all races, *tout court*. At the same time, however, being sensitive to the danger of anachronism also means taking care not to impose narratives of superiority or supremacy onto any and every mention of racial identity from the past.

---

45. John Ruskin, *The Complete Works of John Ruskin Volume XXXIII*, edited by E. T. Cook and A. Wedderburn (London: George Allen & Unwin, 1903–12), pp. 422–3.

46. Peter Ackroyd, *Albion: The Origins of the English Imagination* (London: Vintage Press, 2004), p. 36; Winder, *The Last Wolf*, p. 5.

47. Langford, *Englishness*, p. 9.

48. Nikolaus Pevnser, *The Englishness of English Art* (London: Penguin Books, 1964).

49. Roger Scruton, *England: An Elegy* (London: Continuum, 2006), p. 7.

When it comes to Newman's own comments on race, both of these factors are crucial. Awkwardly for those sympathetic to the 'mongrel' interpretations of Englishness, Newman himself makes frequent reference to the English as 'Saxons', speaking of an ascendant Catholicism in *Difficulties* as the faith 'extending in the great Anglo-Saxon race',[50] for example, or his distinguishing between the English and 'the old Highlanders' who 'if placed on the broad plains of England, would have in time run through their natural existence'.[51] There is no evidence that Newman shared an interpretation of Englishness like that described by Langford, Ackroyd, and Winder. However, it is equally true that, when Newman speaks of race, there are no grounds to suggest he understood any race as superior to others, and there is indeed plentiful evidence to suggest he was generally critical of such assumptions. Of particular relevance here are his criticisms of Charles Boileau Elliott's *Travels in the Three Great Empires of Austria, Russia, and Turkey* in a review from the British Critic published in 1839, prior to Newman's conversion.[52] Here, Newman shares his frustration that Elliot writes with such 'annoyance, dejection, or contempt when he meets with things and persons moulded upon a different standard'. Elliot's self-confidence in English supremacy is deeply distasteful to Newman, his 'appreciation of the worth of every thing of English manufacture'. Indeed, his prejudices towards other peoples is condemned as 'rude, course, and indelicate'.[53]

In the *Present Position*, moreover, Newman alludes to his encounters with foreignness by saying that everyone 'is apt to consider his own view of things, his own principles, his own tastes, to be just and right, and to despise others all together', and this is 'true of nations' and helps explain the 'weak point of Protestantism' in England, that is, it has not appreciated how things look to the eyes of others.[54] Such views of course led him to criticize unthinking and uncritical patriots as 'anglo-maniacs' or 'John Bull-ists'.[55]

It should also be stated that Newman makes various allusions to something close to Ackroyd's focus on the interrelationship of land and identity, albeit without connecting this to 'mongrel' interpretations of race. In one of his letters he even shares his belief in *'genii locorum'*, a concept Ackroyd himself finds helpful for his

---

50. Newman, *Difficulties*, p. 328; there are a great many other examples of Newman calling the English 'saxons' throughout his corpus.

51. John Henry Newman, *Discussions and Arguments* (New York: Longmans, Green, 1907), p. 333.

52. John Henry Newman, 'Elliot's Travels', *British Critic*, vol. 25 (April 1839), pp. 305–20. A possible exception to Newman's equanimity on issues of race and culture is his relationship to Judaism, see Rowan Williams's introduction to *Arians of the Fourth Century* (Leominster: Gracewing, 2001).

53. Newman, 'Elliot's Travels', pp. 306 and 316.

54. Newman, *Present Position*, p. 6.

55. Ibid., p. 26.

own ends.[56] Interestingly, in Newman's extensive critiques of the English character of mind in the *Present Position*, he argues that there are 'First Principles' within all people which define 'innate common sense' and are 'sovereign, irresponsible, and secret'. He says some of these are 'imprinted on the human mind by its Maker', but others 'are common to external localities' so 'men catch them from each other, by education, by daily intercourse, by reading the same books' and so on. Notice that race does not appear here, but place; these First Principles are 'common to external localities', although Newman does not suppose (like Ackroyd) that the localities themselves define those principles, as such. But he maintains that 'nations have very frequently one and same set of First Principles' which are the 'opinion of nearly everyone else' there.[57]

This discussion of the difficulties with Englishness strengthen the benefits to speaking of a 'sensibility' from the previous section. Not only does sensibility best capture the unreflective tenor of terms like 'genius', 'temper', and 'manners', it also avoids an overtly racial designation. That is, like Ackroyd's other favoured term, 'the English imagination', it can be participated in by people of various races, whereas a term like 'genius' smacks of the sort of biological dimension which is untenable today.

2.3 Three aspects of the English sensibility

Having established that the suppositions of an English sensibility are common in Newman's day, along with some of the parameters of this phrase and the difficulties it involves, I can now investigate the content of this English sensibility. David Simpson writes that the Restoration of 1660 not only 'brought with it a visible increase in the rhetoric of national identity' but that this rhetoric assumed that being English 'involved a commitment to common sense, to an ethic of compromises, and a respect for special circumstances rather than adherence to general rules'.[58] The first and third of these commitments will be discussed shortly, whereas here I will focus on the supposed 'ethic of compromises'. The developments in English identity in the century and a half following the Restoration were of course intensified significantly when England was increasingly defined in contrast to France, and the ethics of compromise is no exception. Simpson writes that, in contrast to common sense and compromise, Frenchmen were characterized with

---

56. John Henry Newman, *The Letters and Diaries of John Henry Newman: Volume III: New Bearings: January 1832 to June 1833*, edited by I. Ker and T. Gornall (Oxford: Clarendon Press, 1979). Interestingly, Peter Ackroyd explores the notion of *genius loci* in his lecture 'The Englishness of English Literature', quoted by Merlin Coverley in *Psychogeography* (Hertfordshire: Oldcastle Books, 2006), p. 34.

57. Ibid., pp. 276–8.

58. Simpson, 'Romanticism', pp. 2–3.

'a schizophrenic and unpredictable oscillation between extremes of passionate sensibility and cold-hearted logicality'.[59]

Favouring compromise over extremes, fanaticism, and division is of course not merely about avoiding oscillations in the interiority of individual persons. It has its locus classicus in the intermingling of Protestant and Catholic elements in the Elizabethan settlement obviously, along with combining Parliamentarian and Monarchical government when the settlement was restored in 1660. Such examples underpin Edmund Burke's writing on the unwritten and organically developing constitution, but the link with individual poise is not severed. For Burke, 'our antagonist is our helper', and, as put by Raymond Williams, 'a man's antagonist is in certain aspects himself'.[60] More fundamentally though, Burke's dictum suggests we should seek to accommodate real adversaries, for 'the connexion between the quality of this process [of accommodating adversaries] in individuals and the quality of civil society is major and indisputable'.[61]

Burke's organic view of civil development is closely linked to the process of accommodating difficulties: 'by a slow but well-sustained progress, the effort of each step is watched; the good or ill success of the first gives light to us in the second ... [o]ne advantage is as little as possible sacrificed to another'. In summary, 'we compensate, we reconcile, we balance'.[62] Such a view of Englishness as characterized by reconciling extremes and balance was by 1867–8 to reappear in the work of a younger contemporary of Newman, Matthew Arnold. Arnold's *Culture and Anarchy* presents the English as a balanced combination of two opposing tendencies, the Celtic and the Saxon. He considers Celtic traditions to exemplify 'a passionate, turbulent, indomitable reaction against the disposition of fact' and the Saxon to be 'disciplinable' and 'practical' and therefore 'spreading its exertions within a bounded field, the field of plain sense'. Arnold therefore famously concludes that 'no people ... are so shy, so self-conscious, so embarrassed as the English, because two natures are mixed in them, and natures which pull them in such different ways'.[63]

Indeed, mentions of Englishness as evincing an ethic of compromise remain common long into the twentieth and even the twenty-first centuries. Nikolaus Pevsner, in the immediate post-war period, wrote that the English tendency to favour 'wise compromises' explains 'the two party system not shaken by communism or fascism, the democratic system of negotiation in Parliament' and an English 'distrust' of both 'the sweeping statement' and 'the demagogue'.[64] Peter Ackroyd roots this tendency back even farther than the Restoration, claiming

---

59. Ibid., p. 3.

60. Edmund Burke, *Reflections on the Revolutions in France* (Oxford: Oxford University Press, 1950), pp. 184–5.

61. Williams, *Culture and Society*, pp. 5–6.

62. Burke, *Reflections*, pp. 184–5.

63. Matthew Arnold, *The Study of Celtic Literature* (London: Smith, Elder, 1891), p. 112.

64. Nikolaus Pevsner, *The Englishness of English Art* (London: Penguin Books, 1964), p. 20.

that the language of Middle English itself shows that 'it is in the nature of English literature precisely to reside' at a 'nodal point where two languages or peoples meet'.[65] He also claims William of Malmesbury's commendation of moderation in all things (the 'best is ever mete') shows how medieval English Catholicism evinces a continuous tradition of 'common sense and instinct for compromise'.[66] Ackroyd goes on to include Shakespeare within this broad tendency, as a master of 'the play of oppositions'. As Samuel Johnson noted, Shakespeare wrote plays which are strictly speaking neither 'tragedies nor comedies … [but which mingle both] with endless variety of proportion'. He thus takes issue with Tolstoy's criticisms of Shakespeare's authorial lack of feeling by claiming that 'Shakespeare "feels" only through the medium of contrast, just as he holds no settled opinion except within the play of oppositions.' After all, 'Lear cannot be imagined without the Fool any more than the Fool can be perceived without the presence of Lear.'[67] That is, reality or truth is found by balancing between extremes, it emerges in the interplay between oppositions. Stefan Collini notes that commemorations of the 1688 Glorious Revolution in 1988 left 'the official invocation of the virtues of constitutional compromise and peaceful change' unchallenged.[68] Robert Winder has recently claimed that this Englishness is best described as 'a method, an approach, a set of habitual responses … a *knack*' for 'negotiating a path between extremes', and 'tip-toeing between contrary urges'.[69]

This tendency can be seen in George Herbert's poetry, for example. Newman's friend Hurrell Froude said Herbert has a 'depth of feeling' which his words are not trying to describe, but endeavouring rather to 'conceal', as if the central essence of a thing is an unseen mean between interacting expressions.[70] Herbert's caution about crassly emotive language is rooted in the sense of balance evinced by one who is ever ready to compromise, repelled by fanatical extremes, and favouring moderation in all things. Herbert's poem *The Familie* makes this point:

First peace and silence all disputes controll,
Then Order plaies the soul,
And giving all things their set forms and houres,
Makes of wild woods sweet walks and bowres.[71]

---

65. Ackroyd, *Albion*, pp. 98–9.
66. Ibid., p. 127.
67. Ibid., p. 228.
68. Collini, *English Pasts*, p. 11.
69. Robert Winder, *The Last Wolf: The Hidden Springs of Englishness* (London: Little Brown Group, 2017), p. 416.
70. Edward Short, *Newman and His Contemporaries* (London: T&T Clark Continuum), p. 26.
71. George Herbert, *The Poems of George Herbert* (Oxford: Oxford University Press, 1961), p. 127.

Compromise was typically seen as making the 'wild woods' of fanaticism into 'sweet walks and bowres', and Herbert's poem shows that this sense of balance and moderation is deeply linked with another aspect of the English sensibility which is similarly typical of English self-understanding in the nineteenth century, reserve. Indeed, the link between compromise and reserve is crucial for Arnold, as we have seen, for he suggests that shyness and embarrassment are typically English because the Englishman is comprised of contradictory urges. One might even suggest there is reticence or reserve indicated by the unwritten British Constitution. Poetry again comes into view here. Arnold argued that the ability to discern the quality of a poem was best called 'tact'. This ability is not something that can be learned through written rules, 'theoretically deduced', or given as a 'formulated standard'. He describes it as 'an intuitive faculty developed by the habitual contemplation of the best passages in the best writings'.[72] Paul Langford's sources, broadly contemporary with Newman, record 'tacitunity' as something widely acknowledged as lying close 'to the essence' of the English, who had 'a reputation of being a silent people', being 'less loquacious than their Continental neighbours', and more 'fearful' than others about 'wasting words'.[73] With his much broader time frame, Ackroyd claims to find 'understatement' even in Beowulf, Chaucer, and John Gower, whom another commentator notes exhibits a 'typically English' use of 'unemphatic understatement'.[74] In the mid-twentieth century Pevsner wrote, with a typically German observation given his native tongue's propensity for the multisyllabic compound noun, that 'English is a language aspiring to the monosyllable', which he explains in terms of favouring 'understatement, the aversion against fuss, the distrust of rhetoric'.[75]

Pevsner's 'distrust of rhetoric' observation is related to another aspect of reserve, the distrust of theory. Arnold's 'tact' offers a way to discern poetic quality that cannot be theorized. This distrust of theory is also closely related to a third aspect of Englishness: 'empiricism'. Simpson argues that, following from 1660, the English tradition 'had been belligerently empiricist' long 'before the French Revolution'. As we have seen, this empiricism includes a commitment to 'common sense' and 'a respect for special circumstances rather than adherence to general rules'. General rules are the domain of theory, 'special circumstances' belong to the domain of empirical reality. The unwritten – as in untheorized – constitution is again central to this aspect of English self-understanding: in 'happy contradiction of the French' its 'glory' was said 'to consist in its having no theory, in its being the gradual and patient accumulation of practice and precedent'.[76] The widespread condemnation of 'theory' one encounters in English writers like Arthur Young

---

72. Matthew Arnold, *Essays in Criticism: Second Series* (London: Macmillan, 1935), pp. 5 and 14. See also Simpson, 'Romanticism', p. 6.
73. Langford, *Englishness Identified*, pp. 175–6.
74. Quoted by Ackroyd, *Albion*, pp. xx, 159, 161 n.13.
75. Pevsner, *Englishness*, p. 17.
76. Simpson, 'Romanticism', p. 2.

is not anti-intellectualism per se but a favouring of drawing conclusions from 'experience' as something which makes such conclusions different from 'unEnglish' intellectualism, that is, 'French theory'.[77] As put by Langford, 'even when they sought to generalize, the English seemed incapable of abandoning their boastful empiricism', for 'theory was for other nations'.[78]

On the most basic level, empiricism describes a disposition whereby concrete reality, the living embodied present, is the primary site of reference rather than holding that ideas, or noetically 'tidy' notions are primary. Fuseli thus commented on the English that their 'tastes and feelings all go to realities'.[79] Collini thus speaks of an English 'disdain for theory', and E. P. Thompson of the English 'empirical idiom' maintains that 'minds that thirst for tidy platonism soon become impatient with actual history'.[80] We have in this connection also what Ackroyd describes in connection with Arnold as the contention that the Saxons have an 'empirical genius', and the tendency of English prose always to avoid 'abstract learning' as exemplified in Thomas Browne's eschewing of any 'ontology or metaphysic'.[81] Indeed, Ackroyd connects this with English religion, claiming this explains why there 'has never been in England a tradition of theological speculation in the manner of an Augustine or an Aquinas'.[82]

Many will associate the term 'empiricism' with the school of philosophy called 'British Empiricism'. There is an obvious connection here, insofar as this school does share the same orientation to the living, physical world that commentators like Thompson consider an idiom of Englishness. However, the term 'empiricism' for this book means something much broader than one particular philosophical school, and indeed some members of that school have tended towards ways of thinking which are antithetical to the original empirical orientation, becoming speculative and idealist.[83] To consider empiricism a typical mode of English philosophy should rather be rooted in basic contentions going back at least as far as William of Ockham, who believed that 'all knowledge is derived from experience', and is surely closely related to Francis Bacon and the scientific revolution.[84]

Speaking of empiricism as a broad orientation to the empirical world rather than primarily a discrete philosophical school diverges from James Cameron's

---

77. Arthur Young, *The Example of France a Warning to Britain* (Dublin, 1793), pp. 32 and 79.

78. Langford, *Englishness Identified*, p. 76.

79. Ibid., p. 31.

80. Collini, *English Pasts*, p. 5 and E. P. Thompson, 'The Peculiarities of the English', in *The Socialist Register*, pp. 311–62.

81. Ackroyd, *Albion*, pp. 11 and 59.

82. Ibid., p. 127.

83. See David Berman, 'George Berkeley', in *Routledge History of Philosophy Volume V: British Empiricism and the Enlightenment*, edited by Stuart Brown (London: Taylor & Francis, 2003), pp. 101–22.

84. Quoted by Ackroyd, *Albion*, p. 128 n.10.

interpretation of Newman as a theological counterpart to British empiricist philosophy. Cameron studies Newman's relationship with English or British Empiricism at great length, and interprets the empirical sentiment of his work as a proximity to the philosophical school of empirical philosophy, calling him the 'apostle of common sense'.[85] However, Cameron's reasoning is that Newman himself was both practical and fanciful: as one who 'established an alliance between the two apparently antagonistic principles of quietism and shrewd common sense – a sort of Benjamin Franklin graft upon a Fenelon stem'.[86] His analysis is thus not so much about the theology (which is included in the 'shrewd common sense' part of Newman's oeuvre) but more about his personality: considering him to have been outwardly empirical yet lapsing into the sort of speculation typical of the empirical idealists. Newman's relationship to British Empiricism will be discussed in Chapters 5, 8, and 11, but suffice to say this book is focused on the theology itself, where no flights of introspective fancy are to be found.

There are two elements of the empirical disposition or orientation which are, by contrast, certainly found in Newman's theological work. The first of these is what can be termed 'pragmatism', and it is closely linked to the British Constitution, again, and similarly found in the writings of Burke. This pragmatism or prudence is displayed by Burke's aforementioned comment that 'we compensate, we reconcile, we balance', that is, opting for piecemeal adjustments to social and civic matters, favouring stability and order over against those 'radical blueprints for social change' associated with events in France. For this reason, 'prudence' is described by Burke as 'the primary virtue of civil government', and any reform is not 'a change in the substance' of the object 'but a direct application of a remedy to the grievance complained of'.[87] English common law is central to this, too, itself also witnessing the 'gradual accumulation of practice and precedent'. Easthope points out that even the Normal Conquest did not cause England to acquire a 'written legal code', or set of principles grounded in theory, and that the endurance of common law 'helps to explain the origins of the English tradition as empiricist'.[88] Common law is also connected by Scruton with the notion of Englishness being rooted in the land rather than the people. It was, he points out, the 'law of the land', meaning

---

85. See Jacob Phillips, 'John Henry Newman and the English Sensibility', *Logos; A Journal of Catholic Thought and Culture*, vol. 24, no. 3 (2021): 108–29. As put by Cameron in 'Apostle', 'empiricism as a philosophical doctrine seems both hard-headed and fanciful, to emphasise immediate experience and yet construct vast imaginative pictures'. He sees in this school a 'tendency' to 'tempt inquirers into a maze of sophistry and illusion'. Newman is caught up to some extent in proximity to both aspects of this school, for Cameron. In 'having this dual character' he writes empiricism 'seems almost tailored to fit Newman'. That is, Newman is not only both practical and industrious but also given to endless introspection, pathos, and poetic spirituality, as one who said as a child 'I thought life might be like a dream', pp. 42–59.

86. Stephen Newsome, quoted by James M. Cameron in 'Apostle', p. 44.

87. Williams, *Culture and Society*, pp. 4–5 and 7.

88. Easthope, *Englishness*, p. 27.

law as it applied to a distinctive place. Common law is also connected with the prudential wisdom of 'common sense'. Pevsner comes to mind here, again, for he speaks of the 'more permanent quality' of the English, as 'common sense or reason'.[89] Pevsner considers this to be typified by the once-common maxim, 'every case on its own merit'.[90]

The mention of 'common sense' leads to the second aspect of empiricism which will prove important in subsequent chapters, utility or industriousness. During British industrial ascendancy the well-recognized supposition that the English were given to practical reality of course fed into the narrative that the British were particularly industriousness and productive. Hence, Goethe's comment on 'Englishmen' that 'practicality was the "main secret of their ascendency amongst the various races of the earth"'.[91] Langford lists 'practicality' as one of the primary perceived attributes of the English in his sources, which generally agree that 'good common sense' is a 'truly English attribute'.[92] Underlying these assumptions, says Langford, 'was a profound belief in the Englishman as a doer rather than a thinker' who 'always conceived himself as a man of action'.[93] Indeed, Newman himself notes that many have commented on how German theologians have made such 'profound attainments' because the English clergy are 'not a reading body' in reflection of the fact the English are 'an active, not a studious race'.[94]

At the close of this chapter, then, the reasoning behind the phrase 'English sensibility' is established, as are the necessary nuances and limits of this phrase. We now have a suitable basis to take three aspects, compromise, reserve, and empiricism, and study Newman's theological writings to investigate how these aspects impact on the work therein.

---

89. Pevsner, *Englishness*, p. 28.
90. Ibid., p. 67.
91. Langford, *Englishness Identified*, p. 75.
92. Quoted by Langford, *Englishness Identified*, p. 79 n.281.
93. Ibid., p. 81 n.328.
94. John Henry Newman, *Essays Critical and Historical* (London: Longmans, Green, 1907), p. 298.

Chapter 3

NEWMAN'S TRACTARIAN COMPROMISE

Much of Newman's Tractarian thought is rooted in the Caroline Divines, including the English instinct for compromise which is exemplified by the *via media*. This is an Anglican ecclesiological motif with its roots farther back than the Carolines, in Richard Hooker's *Lawes of Ecclesiastical Polity* (1594 and 1597). Hooker presents the Elizabethan settlement as 'the natural and reasonable form of religion for the English people', partly through a 'tone of debate that was reasoned and moderate': a 'measured tranquillity'.[1] This interpretation of Anglicanism gained importance in the work of the Caroline Divines in the seventeenth century. Received notions of compromise as a moderating between extremes, or what Mark Langham calls 'English moderation', when 'combined with a dislike of foreigners' produced 'among many people favourable to the break with Rome a very cautious attitude to the continental Reformation'.[2] In short, they held that there were extreme doctrinal positions pertaining to both Geneva and Rome, to Calvinist and the 'Romanist' theologies, and that the distinctive role of the Church of England was to strike a balance or compromise position between these two. This gave rise to what Matthew Parker spoke of as the 'golden mediocrity' of the English Church.[3]

3.1 Tractarian radical conservatism

The *via media* is dealt with directly by Newman in two of the *Tracts for the Times* from 1834, and then at length in the *Prophetical Office* (1837). In Tract 38, 'Via Media 1', Newman adopts a broadly Caroline position, putting into the mouth of his rhetorical interlocuter, 'Clericus', the words, 'I like foreign interference, as little from Geneva, as from Rome', for 'the glory of the English Church, is that is has taken the VIA MEDIA' and thus 'lies *between* the (so-called) Reformers and the Romanists'. The Tract's primary purpose is to argue that the Church of England

---

1. Mark Langham, *The Caroline Divines and the Church of Rome: A Contribution to Current Ecumenical Dialogue* (London: Routledge, 2018), p. 1, see note 13.
2. Ibid.
3. See T. Holtzen, 'The Anglican Via Media: The Idea of Moderation in Reform', *Journal of Anglican Studies*, vol. 17, no. 1 (2019): 48–73, doi:10.1017/S174035531800027X.

cannot rightly be considered exclusively Protestant. Newman rails against those who think it 'enough to prove an English clergyman unfaithful to his Church' if he is 'at variance with the opinions of the Diet of Augsburg, or the Confessions of the Waldenses'.[4] Prima facie, then, Newman seems to want to conserve and perpetuate the Caroline approach to Anglican ecclesiology as the treading of the *via media*, and apply this approach as a corrective to the evangelicalism which was ascendant in the early nineteenth century.

However, Newman's Tractarianism is not merely restorative or conservative, but something innovative or radical as well. In Tract 41, 'Via Media No. 2', his second rhetorical interlocuter, Laicus, is shocked at Clericus's radicalism when he calls for 'a second Reformation'. Like the Reformation proper, says Clericus, this will re-establish the Church of England on its proper foundations, because 'the Church has in a measure forgotten its own principles, as declared in the 16th Century'.[5] In short, Newman envisaged that the return or renewal of the *via media* in Anglican self-understanding would be as seismic for the English as the continental reform was for Christendom. Here we see that counter-cultural fervour of the *Tracts* mentioned in Chapter 1. Newman frequently adopts apocalyptic rhetoric to make such points: 'In a day like this there are but two sides, zeal and persecution, the Church and the world', writes Newman in Tract 2, 'The Catholic Church'. He goes on, 'those who attempt to occupy the ground' between the Church and world, will 'at best' lose 'their labour', but more 'probably be drawn back to the latter'.[6] There is certainly no *via media* between Church and world, therefore, and Newman shows no fear of controversy in making this point. Addressing his fellow clergymen directly, he writes, 'for many years, we have been in the habit of resting our claim on the general duties of submission to authority, of decency and order, and respecting precedents long established', but now it is the time to appeal to a far superior 'warrant', the Apostolic Succession, which he says 'marks us, *exclusively*, for GOD'S AMBASSADORS'.[7] It is therefore a case of 'piety' and 'Christian Reverence' and not 'good order and expedience only' which prompts the Tractarians to take 'all earthly risks' in order 'to preserve and transmit the seal and warrant of Christ'.[8]

The counter-cultural fervour displayed in passages like this indicate how the Tractarian Newman seems sometimes to strain against the very tradition he wants to preserve. As mentioned in the previous chapter, expedience is closely related to the pragmatic caution of moderation and compromise, and therefore of the *via*

---

4. *Tracts for the Times Volume One; 1833–1834 Tracts 1–46 and Records of the Church 1–18*, edited by Christopher Poore (Galesburg, IL: Seminary Street Press, 2021), p. 336 (neither the Augsburg nor Waldenses confessions mentioned in this Tract (38) were Swiss Calvinists anyway, but presumably this is a comic, rhetorical flourish on Newman's part).

5. *Tracts*, p. 361.

6. Ibid., p. 13.

7. Ibid., p. 19.

8. Ibid.

media. From the outset of Newman's engaging with the notion of an Anglican *via media*, then, there are elements which are both conservative and radical. He seeks to preserve an established ecclesiological motif, while also putting it to work for radical, transformative ends, a 'second Reformation'.

The Prophetical Office, published three years after the *via media* Tracts, fleshes out his rediscovery of Caroline ecclesiology in much more detail. He now stops referring to Protestantism as 'Geneva', and presents his adversary as English 'popular Protestantism'. The adversary is now in his own land and culture. The advertisement for the book describes this 'popular Protestantism' as 'that generalized idea of religion, now in repute, which merges all differences of faith and principle between Protestants in minor matters' and which is 'at this day the rallying-point of all that is loyal and high-minded in the nation'.[9] Newman takes aim at this foe, at Protestant national self-belief, he claims, for the sake of the Anglican Church, and in the spirit of Bishop John Bramhall (1594–1663). He quotes Bramhall as saying 'no man can justly blame me for honouring my spiritual Mother, the Church of England, in whose womb I was conceived, at whose breast I was nourished, and in whose bosom I hope to die'. Bramhall's words seem to apply to Newman too when we read, 'I have endeavoured to set down the naked truth impartially, without either favour or prejudice'.[10]

This avoiding of both 'favour' and 'prejudice' can be seen in the overall aims of the *Prophetical Office*, which again has radical and conservative elements. That is, he seeks to conserve the 'golden mediocrity' of the English Divines and their presentation of the Church of England's 'distinctive character', while urging a 'second Reformation' to work against tendencies deemed 'high-minded' in the English popular mind.[11] Newman's Tractarian radicalism is now directed not only against 'the world' but more specifically towards an element of English national sentiment, namely, a self-confidence in the rectitude of Protestantism as the 'rallying point of all that is loyal and high-minded in the nation'.

The critiquing of an aspect of Englishness itself is demonstrated by Tractarian reservations towards calling the Anglican Church 'the Church of England'. The concern was that this title suggests this Church is 'of' a mere part of the world, rooted primarily in national territory rather than in God alone. For the Tractarians, the Church of England must recognize that it is exclusively formed and defined by God, not English national sentiment. Thomas Keble thus demands in Tract 12 that people speak rather of 'the Church *in* England', meaning God's universal Church as it exists 'in' the English milieu without being 'of' that milieu. Similarly, Arthur Philip Percival commends his readers to think not of 'the Church of England' but of 'that part of CHRIST'S Church in this Kingdom which is usually called the Church of England'.[12] The Church of England's state privileges are neither here nor

---

9. Newman, *Prophetical Office*, p. xi.
10. Ibid., p. xii.
11. Ibid., pp. 19–20.
12. *Tracts*, pp. 76 and 186.

there, says Bowden in Tract 29, for were it 'to lose its wealth and honour, it would not, could not, cease to be a branch of the true Church' founded solely on the 'rock' that is Jesus Christ.[13]

Yet all this provocation is joined with a marked conservativism, a desire to ensure Anglicanism's tradition is not discarded. As William Palmer writes in Tract 15, the 'English Church' was not led to 'revolt' under the influence of continental reformers during the English Reformation, because such men had 'nothing by succession from the Apostles'. This Church thus has an unbroken line of succession: 'There was no new Church founded among us.'[14] Somewhat surprisingly, then, at times the Tracts seem almost to yearn for the aftermath of the Reformation, as the point when the *via media* came to expression: 'I do take it to be one most conspicuous mark of God's adorable Providence over us ... that Churches in England escaped in that evil day from either extreme', writes Newman in Tract 20. This Tract was published in December 1833, and constitutes the first appearance of the *via media* in his published works. Then, we read, the Church of England was neither 'corrupted doctrinally', meaning it had not surrendered to the supposed aberrations of Rome which preceded the English Reformation, nor 'secularized ecclesiastically', meaning it had not surrendered continuous succession from the Apostles entailing a divinely infused episcopal governance rooted in Christ himself.[15] In the *Prophetical Office* Newman conducts a full-length examination of the *via media*, arguing that 'virtue lies in a mean, in a point, almost invisible to the world, hard to find, acknowledged but by the few'.[16] His task now is to locate this elusive centre and make it visible.

3.2 The radical conservatism of the Prophetical Office

The *Prophetical Office* begins by setting out the need for there to be a lucid and agreed understanding of the word 'Church' because it is included in the Apostle's Creed. Newman states that its inclusion in the Creed entails that 'some meaning was anciently attached to the word', as indeed history testifies that once 'its meaning was indisputed'.[17] This goes right back to the second Tract, where Newman makes the same point in a statement which could serve as a clarion call for the Tractarian movement in toto: 'The one Catholic and Apostolic Church' is given in the Creed 'as a *fact*, and a fact to be *believed*, and therefore practiced'.[18] In other words, to hold that the word Church can encompass a variety of different interpretations each corresponding to variants

---

13. Ibid., p. 272.
14. Ibid., p. 105.
15. Ibid., p. 185.
16. Newman, *Prophetical Office*, p. 41.
17. Ibid., p. 3.
18. *Tracts*, p. 7.

of Anglicanism makes no sense to Newman insofar as the word is included in a creedal statement of belief. Yet, 'there are interminable disputes and hopeless differences about its meaning now', and moreover, some consider this actually advantageous, because they can make their own choices about which parties to offer their allegiance: the 'great mass of educated men' consider it thus fitting to 'their Christian liberty' to have such freedom of choice of essentials of the faith.[19] Here we see a first glimpse of how compromise as the *via media* feeds into notions of the English as 'free born'.

Newman implies that a semantic plurality pertaining to the word Church is a recent aberration, produced by an increasingly rationalistic climate after the Enlightenment. There can no such flexibility when, say, reciting the words in the creed pertaining to the co-equal divinity of the Paraclete or the reality of the Incarnation. Again, Newman is calling for a return to the seventeenth century, seeking to conserve the true Church of England, as a branch of the 'holy, Catholic, and Apostolic Church' of the creeds. He says he wants 'to build-up what man has pulled down', but not through theological inventiveness or what might today be termed 'constructive theology', so much as drawing attention to the Church's own inherent resources, that is, 'by means of the stores of Divine truth bequeathed to us in the works of our standard English authors'.[20] What is required is a reminder that 'the English Church has a mission', and that is to be 'Catholic but not Roman'. Therefore, 'her members should be on the watch for bringing-out and carrying into effect' this 'distinctive character'.[21]

Importantly however, this 'distinctive character' is described by Newman as intrinsically linked to Englishness itself, notwithstanding the desire to highlight the threat of Christ's Church being subsumed by its English identity. Imagining Rome gaining ground in England against some point in the future, Newman envisages a situation whereby Romanists and Protestants deliver 'forth solemn anathemas upon each other in the name of the Lord!'. But here, 'English theology would come in with its characteristic calmness and caution, clear and decided in its view, giving no encouragement to lukewarmness or liberalism, but withholding all absolute anathemas as errors of opinion, except where the primitive Church makes use of them'.[22] This 'characteristic calmness and caution' is arguably more reflective of received notions of a national sensibility than it is of Scripture and Tradition. A similar moment is found with Newman's comment that the *via media* 'partakes of that indeterminateness, which is to a certain extent the characteristic of English theology'.[23] So far, then, the *Prophetical Office* might seem largely conservative, seeking to reorient Anglicanism upon Caroline sources and the distinctive character of the English sensibility.

19. Ibid.
20. Newman, *Prophetical Office*, p. 5.
21. Ibid., pp. 19–20.
22. Ibid., p. 21.
23. Ibid., p. 129.

At the same time, however, despite Newman's claims about wanting to uncover 'the stores of Divine truth bequeathed to us in the works of our standard English authors', he engages in much constructive theological work in the *Prophetical Office*, and does so in ways which are strikingly innovative and daring, that is, radical. He says he seeks to outline 'a positive doctrine' for the *via media*, transforming it from an indeterminate motif into a concrete set of commitments, making it 'clear and decided in its view'. Because the creed asserts belief in the Church, 'Christians especially need and have a right to require' a 'positive doctrine' of what the word Church means, and this definition needs to be 'definite and intelligible'.[24] There 'is a vast inheritance' he says of the English divines, 'but no inventory of our treasures', so 'it remains to us to catalogue, sort, distribute, select, harmonize, and complete' them.[25] Despite the conservatism at play then, Newman is boldly setting out an inventive agenda which will transform the old Caroline *via media* into something new.

3.3 The tensions of the Prophetical Office

There are points in the *Prophetical Office* where the combination of conservative and radical elements threatens to result in significant tensions. Specifically, Newman struggles to maintain consistency while celebrating both the 'indeterminateness' of English theology while at the same time advancing a 'positive doctrine' by which the *via media* might be rendered 'clear and determined'. On one hand, Newman presents 'indeterminateness' as a characteristically English element to Anglican theology, and one that has much to commend it, not least with its 'characteristic calmness and caution' serving as antidote to the cacophony of 'solemn anathemas' ever voiced by Rome and the Protestants.[26] Leaving things undetermined is thus connected with the avoidance of party allegiances, extremes, and fanaticism, as is the general tenor of the 'instinct for compromise' discussed in the previous chapter. In the third lecture of the work, on The Doctrine of Infallibility Morally Considered, this affection for 'indeterminateness' is raised to something much more significant, something with genuine theological substance, even.

This lecture presents the Roman position on infallibility as 'secured upon two conditions', namely, that 'there be a God, "who cannot lie"' who is the 'source of Revelation' and that the Church is 'infallible to convey' that Revelation.[27] As mentioned above, Newman presents the Anglican position as following a pattern 'according to English principles', that 'religious faith has all it needs in having only the former of these two secured to it, in knowing that God is our Creator and Preserver, and that He *may*, if it so happen, have spoken'.[28] The indeterminateness

---

24. Ibid., p. 6.
25. Ibid., p. 29.
26. Ibid., p. 21.
27. Ibid., p. 86.
28. Ibid., see note 6.

hangs on the subjunctive 'may', for Newman maintains that there is a range of things about God of which God himself has not spoken directly, and the Church of England not having an infallible oracle on earth is thus left with a great number of indeterminate things. Newman maintains that there are significant ethical consequences (or 'moral' considerations), and these take up most of the discussion. He outlines two corollaries of this indeterminateness which are particularly salient for this discussion insofar as we see in each of them that what is, by Newman's own admission, an aspect of the English sensibility in 'indeterminateness', gives theological and doctrinal substance to his theology.

The first corollary is that the practical decision-making of Christians is actually greatly advantaged, in moral terms, if it does not simply submit to some external authority. This is described as both the 'trial' and the 'praise' of the English approach, in which the Christian must 'hang upon the thought' of Christ and not upon 'infallible informants', thus having 'to act in the way which seems on the whole most likely to please Him'.[29] Roman infallibility is presented as authoritarian, and invariably slipping into legalism, for to 'require such definitive and clear notions of truth, is to hanker after the Jewish law'.[30] Such legalism is problematic primarily because it downgrades the mystery of God, for the Jewish law is said by Newman to be 'a system of less mysterious information than Christianity'.[31] But acknowledging God as mystery takes this discussion far beyond 'English principles', and is of course for Newman something at the very core of what it is to be Christian. Not having explicit directives means to live in an 'unconscious devotion' to the Lord. Whereas, for the Roman, 'each deed as its price, every quarter of the land of promise is laid down and described'.[32] 'Unconscious devotion' fosters the 'delicacy and generous simplicity of our obedience', however. Indeed, Newman goes so far as to say that when everything is determined, 'Christian holiness ... loses its freshness, vigour, and comeliness, being frozen (as it were) into certain attitudes, which are not graceful except when they are unstudied'.[33]

The second 'moral' corollary is closely related to this, and involves the indeterminateness of English principles precluding the possibility of an exhaustive theological system. On this front, Newman says it is a 'peculiarity of the Roman system' to which this determinate 'temper gives rise',[34] that the Roman Church 'is obliged to profess a complete knowledge of the whole Dispensation, such as the Apostles had not'.[35] Again, moreover, determinateness threatens mystery, and as such, there is an intrinsic relation between an 'English principle' and a central facet of Christianity itself. He writes, 'that feeling of awe which the mysteriousness

---

29. Ibid., p. 86.
30. Ibid., p. 88.
31. Ibid.
32. Ibid., p. 104.
33. Ibid.
34. Ibid., p. 88.
35. Ibid., p. 89.

of the Gospel should excite, fades away under [a] fictitious illumination which is poured over the entire Dispensation', and again, this 'destroys the delicacy and reverence of the Christian mind'.[36]

For both moral corollaries to English indeterminateness, Newman presents something in keeping with the English sensibility as intrinsic to the faith, almost indistinguishable from it. We see much the same impulse in Tract 45, where Newman launches a similar attack against 'Geneva', as a tendency which makes Scripture 'the sole document for ascertaining and proving our faith'. This is said to give rise to always requiring 'a standard of proof simulating demonstration'. However, 'in the course of time, all the delicate shades of truth and falsehood … the low tones of the "still small voice" in which Scripture abounds, were rudely rejected'. He gives numerous examples from Scripture of people acting without explicit instruction, like Lydia of Acts, as alternatives to those whom 'Our Saviour' condemned for always wanting a sign, analogous to something determinate. To determine everything is to be like those the Psalmist describes as 'needing bridle and bit'.[37]

Given this admiration for indeterminateness, therefore, it is all the more surprising that the entire modus operandi of the *Prophetical Office* is precisely to *determine* the substance of the *via media*. Newman is clear about there being an urgent need to outline what this doctrine involves, and not leave the details of it 'unstudied' in the name of God's mysterious providence. This is absolutely necessary, he says, for if 'we begin by saying that the English doctrine is not at present embodied in any substantive form' and leave it at that, 'we seem content to reduce religion to mere literature, to make reason the judge of it, and to confess it a matter of opinion'.[38] That the *via media* threatens to be reduced to 'mere literature' is highly instructive here. This means it threatens to become just sensibility, and thus to neglect its God-given theological character. Newman thus seeks to give theological grounds for an aspect of Englishness, so it can be acknowledged as more than mere Englishness.

The same impulse is displayed as regards private judgement. Here, notwithstanding his prior praising of indeterminateness, Newman says the 'middle path' between absolutizing private judgement in Protestantism, and its wholesale rebuttal in Romanism, is disadvantageous to belief. He says the hitherto undetermined nuances of the Anglican approach to private judgement cannot 'easily be mastered by the mind' precisely because of its 'indeterminateness'. The answer, he writes, is 'to give it something more of meaning and reality than it popularly possesses'.[39] Again, Newman explicitly seeks determinateness, or at least to determine the parameters of indeterminateness.

---

36. Ibid., p. 91.
37. *Tracts*, pp. 403–4.
38. Newman, *Prophetical Office*, p. 22.
39. Ibid., p. 130.

Newman's argumentation threatens to cancel itself out. That is, he praises indeterminateness yet claims that determination is required to avoid doctrine becoming 'mere literature'. He thus enunciates six steps to the *via media* of private judgement. These are, as follows: (1) 'Scripture, Antiquity, and Catholicity cannot contradict each other', (2) 'when the Moral Sense of the individual' contradicts Scripture, 'we must follow Scripture', (3) 'that when the sense of Scripture, as interpreted by the Reason of the individual, is contrary to the sense given to it by Catholic Antiquity, we ought to side with the latter', (4) that 'in important matters' we must follow Antiquity over the present Church, and vice versa 'in unimportant matters', (5) that 'when the present Church speaks contrary to our private notions, and Antiquity is silent … it is pious to sacrifice our own opinion to that of the Church', and finally (6) 'if, in spite of our efforts to agree with the church, we still differ from it, Antiquity being silent, we must avoid causing any disturbance, recollecting that the Church, not individuals, "has authority in controversies of faith"'.[40] So, Newman previously argued that indeterminateness is vital to Christian holiness, and is emblematic of the mystery of God due to its unsystematic character, but his analysis only applies within the space left for private judgement after it has been established that neither Scripture nor Antiquity has spoken on the matter, and that the matter is simply unimportant and insignificant, after having followed six clearly delineated steps in the process of discernment. In other words, this does not seem to leave very much room for indeterminateness at all, and very little in the way of the spacious compromising between anathemas that left the English free to trust their own minds in discerning what is to be done.

We see a similar tension when it comes to Newman's praising of Anglican theology's distinctively English 'unsystematic' character. In a review of William Palmer's *Treatise on the Church of Christ*, in an edition of the *British Critic* from 1838, he moves towards favouring system, although the *Prophetical Office* spoke of 'system' as that which will 'pour' a 'fictitious illumination' over 'the entire Dispensation' and thus destroy the 'reverence of the Christian mind'.[41] Newman presents Palmer's book as exceptional among Anglican theological works, for it sets out to offer a complete theological textbook and not merely an occasional response to a contemporary controversy. Newman's review lists various advantages and disadvantages to the unsystematic character of the Anglican divines, giving more attention to the negative consequences. He says, 'if an inquirer be ill-disposed to receive what he reads' the 'absence of method and order' that an unsystematic theological corpus involves 'will greatly strengthen his prejudice against it'. If various facts and propositions are mutually enforcing in a cohesive structure, however, or 'when all the parts mutually support and are supported', we will find that 'we have a phantasia of truth forced upon our minds, even against our will'. The 'persuasiveness' of a cohesive system rests in the fact it appears to

---

40. Ibid., p. 137. The inverted commas would suggest this is a quotation, but it is uncited by Newman, as was common practice in most of his works.

41. Ibid., p. 91.

the enquirer 'that various phenomena, found together, and withal consistent and uniform, do belong, and therefore do witness, to some one real principle existing as the cause of them'.

Newman thus concludes that mutually enforcing facts and propositions working in harmony in disclosing the fundamentals of a system will combine and conspire towards making those fundamentals all the more convincing as objective truths. 'English theology and English treatises,' however, 'are deficient in this internal presumption of truth' because they are at best 'partially systematic'. Here, Newman strikes a very different note to that of Lecture III of the *Prophetical Office*, where he criticizes the systematic exhaustiveness of the 'Roman system'. A year later he has decided that Anglicanism needs to be much more exhaustive, as indeed are 'Calvinism' and 'Romanism', for it is a great detriment to the Church of England that it has never attained 'a theory ... capable of accounting for all questions'.[42]

3.4 Summary

This chapter demonstrates that Newman's Tractarian writings share the instinct for compromise of the English sensibility through their consistent focus on the *via media*, particularly in the *Prophetical Office*. This text also celebrates aspects of compromise impacting on theology as reflective of the English sensibility – particularly the 'calmness and caution' of indeterminateness, which is held to be morally beneficial for enabling people to avoid legalism and safeguard God as mystery. At the same time however, there are significant tensions at play insofar as Newman explicitly seeks to determine the parameters of the *via media*, and adumbrate the space between Rome and 'Popular Protestantism', to such a degree that it undermines the very same benefits he associates with indeterminateness itself. As it stands, then, Newman seems to be caught up in Englishness while also straining against it. This tension stems from the fact he seems to give an element of Englishness to some theological authority as avoiding legalism and safeguarding mystery, while at the same time wanting to highlight the dangers of confusing national sentiment with religion – of rendering the English Church as being 'of' England not 'in' it, and of expressing all that is 'loyal and high-minded in the nation' rather than God himself.

42. John Henry Newman, 'Palmer's Treatise on the Church of Christ', *British Critic*, vol. 24 (October 1838): 182–3.

Chapter 4

NEWMAN'S TRACTARIAN RESERVE

The English 'instinct for compromise' is closely linked to the second aspect of the English sensibility to be discussed here: 'reserve'. Compromise is linked to reserve through moderation, as in a moderating between extremes. As we shall see, this was held to give rise to a controlled and thoughtful manner of written or spoken expression, and entails a corresponding distaste or disdain for unduly bold or overbearing speech.[1] As with the *via media* moreover, the roots of Newman's Tractarian reserve are found in the writings of the Caroline Divines, who are traditionally seen as supreme examples of a 'civility and urbanity of language'.[2] This urbanity was not merely aesthetic, however, but connected with a sense of caution and a corresponding propriety of speech in relation to the divine. The Carolines had followed in the path of Hooker, who criticized theologians for their incautious and overly bold statements over the precise mechanics of the Eucharistic change, for example. Intemperate language follows from extremities of outlook, and so Hooker chastises those who 'vainly trouble' themselves with 'fierce contentions'.[3] A temperate or reserved use of language towards the Sacrament was thus seen by Herbert Thorndike, for example, as indicative of a proper disposition of reverence and devotion for matters deemed unutterably holy.[4] The Tractarian Newman inherits these two aspects to reserve, both admiring a temperate use of language

---

1. In a letter to Charles Newman in March 1825, John Henry writes, 'you are in an unquiet state of mind altogether at variance with the calm, equable, candid, philosophical temper which [is] necessary for balancing ... and adjusting such difficult questions as many of those connected with religion'. This 'heated state of mind' he goes on, explains Charles's 'intemperate language'. John Henry Newman, *The Letters and Diaries of John Henry Cardinal Newman: Vol. I: Ealing, Trinity, Oriel, February 1801 to December 1826*, edited by I. Ker and T. Gornall (Oxford: Clarendon Press, 1979), pp. 212–13.
2. Langham, *Caroline Divines*, p. 21.
3. Quoted by ibid., p. 31, see note 11.
4. Ibid., p. 33, see note 26.

which issues from a moderate temper of mind, and use of language which is cautious and reserved in reflection of the awesome sanctity of the divine.[5]

4.1 Background to Arians

Reserve is an important theme of Newman's Tractarian theology, and this is shown most extensively in *Arians* (1833), a work broadly representative of Newman's thinking at least in his earlier Tractarian years. The book was written on invitation, and initially intended for Rivington's Theological Library. Newman records in his diary that he finished the work on 31 July 1832. In October of that year, the publisher William Rowe Lyall wrote to Hugh James Rose praising the work, but suggesting its constructive character means it would be better to publish it independently from the series. Interestingly, he says 'the style' is something 'I like particularly: it is thoroughly *English*'.[6] Insofar as there was a recognized tendency to reserve afoot in perceptions of an alleged English sensibility during this period, however, the Englishness of *Arians* goes far beyond just the prose style.

The overall intention of the work reflects a particular theological difficulty for the theologians who would later become known as the Oxford Movement. They needed to reconnect the Anglican Church with the early Church of the Creeds and Councils, or what they called 'the primitive Church'. One difficulty with this, however, was establishing a robust rationale for maintaining that the Church of England must adhere to the early Catholic Tradition, yet not adhere to later Catholic Tradition, or what would be considered 'Roman aberrations' of the primitive faith.

The classical Anglican view was associated with the dictum of St Vincentius of Lérins that 'Christianity is what has been held always, everywhere and by all.'[7] This meant that the faith of the primitive Church was paramount, existing prior to significant separations and schisms, or at least prior to any breakaway group that could rightly bear the name of Christian. In stark contrast to the Lérins dictum, there was an approach associated with the Tridentine-era Catholic Church, which held Roman authority to be the only seal of truth and authenticity against all the schismatic and splintering Christian groups past and present. These two approaches can be applied to discussions of the Arian controversy. For the classical Anglican view, there is Richard Hooker, who argued that although pre-fourth-century sources might not use the language of Christ being 'begotten not made', that nevertheless 'the faith of the early councils has been present in a recognisable form ... since New Testament times ... [but] the technical language ... took time

---

5. John Keble seems to have been particularly influential on the Tractarian affection for reserve, as is brought out effectively by Edward Short in *Newman and His Contemporaries*, pp. 28–30.
6. Newman, *Letters and Diaries III*, pp. 104–5.
7. See Cameron, in Newman, *Development*, p. 74.

to develop'.[8] So, Nicaea corresponds with 'what has been held always, everywhere and by all', presumably implying that, for Hooker, the same could not be said of the formal definition of Transubstantiation. On the other hand, the interpretation of scholars like Dionysius Petavius saw that 'early Christian conceptions' dating from the New Testament times and soon afterwards were 'imprecise' and 'erroneous by later standards' and development was therefore 'only possible through the Magisterium', that is, by virtue of authority.[9]

Newman's challenge was to explain how central elements of the faith like the Nicene Creed had been believed 'always, everywhere and by all' when the historical sources might suggest otherwise, in order to avoid making recourse to authority as definitive in grounding doctrinal authenticity. To do this, he utilizes a relatively obscure element of seventeenth-century patristic scholarship: the '*disciplina arcani*', or 'secret discipline'. This refers to the practice of 'the early Church of concealing certain theological doctrines' from 'catechumens and pagans'.[10] The term *disciplina arcani* itself originates in 1614, and is not now generally taken seriously by early Church historians.[11] The *disciplina arcani* promised to offer Newman the missing link he needed to situate his Anglicanism firmly on the witness of the primitive church. As historical scholarship was making it harder and harder to argue that the authentic doctrines were clearly perceptible in earlier Christianity, one does not want to follow Petavius and rest on authority alone – the alternative is to suggest that there was a sound grasp of Trinitarian doctrine in the early Church, but with stipulations and customs about when and how it might be spoken or written of, thus leaving us with very scant references in the primary sources.

Arians was written during 1822–33, and is therefore not strictly speaking a Tractarian work, for it predates Tract I by some months. Yet it is broadly representative of Tractarian theology, not least through reserve's centrality within it. John Keble's Tract 40 (1834), for example, speaks of being selective in discussing the need to reinstitute ecclesiastical discipline, and using 'a kind of holy reserve towards those who will not hear'.[12] In Newman's Tract 71 (1836), he mirrors exactly what he earlier associates with the *disciplina arcani* of ancient Alexandria, in speaking of the need for Tractarians to debate with Rome in a way which must 'keep clear, as much as possible, of the subjects more especially sacred'. On the Trinity and Incarnation he says, one should not 'invoke the direct contemplation of heavenly things, when one should wish to bow the head and be silent'. He even says the 'Holy Eucharist' cannot 'well be discussed in words at all, without the

---

8. Brian E. Daley, 'The Church Fathers', in *The Cambridge Companion to John Henry Newman*, edited by Ian Ker and Terrence Merrigan (Cambridge: Cambridge University Press, 2009), pp. 29–46, 32.

9. Ibid., pp. 32–3.

10. 'Disciplina arcani', in *The Oxford Dictionary of the Christian Church*, 3rd edn, edited by F. L. Cross and E. A. Livingstone (Oxford: Oxford University Press, 2005), p. 491.

11. Ibid.

12. *Tracts*, p. 348.

sacrifice of "godly fear".[13] Moreover, Isaac Williams authored two Tracts 'On the Principle of Reserve in Communicating Religious Knowledge'. The first, Tract 81, applies the principle to God himself, showing how revelation proceeds gradually, and selectively, being reserved and then dispensed according to Providence. The second, Tract 86, is itself focused on the *disciplina arcani*. One can therefore safely treat *Arians* as a broadly Tractarian text, at least in content.

Arians is difficult to read critically as a work of Church history. It is hardly well-regarded today as a reliably historical account, having been called 'a colossally over schematic treatment of history' by Rowan Williams, and described as 'Newman's first novel' by Stephen Thomas.[14] But importantly for present purposes, Newman freely makes connections between the ante-Nicene Church and the Church of England of the early 1830s, suggesting that regardless of the book's credentials as history, it should still be taken seriously as a work of theology: 'his treatment of Arianism ... is rhetorical' for 'he is trying to persuade his contemporaries of present dangers'.[15] Moreover, these nods to the contemporary English context often centre precisely on reserve. He writes that learning from primitive Christianity will mean much 'mischievous fanaticism is avoided, which *at present* abounds from the vanity of men, who think they can explain the sublime doctrines and exuberant promises of the Gospel' (my italics).[16] Similarly, he states that 'now', meaning during the time of writing, 'we allow ourselves publicly to canvass the most solemn truths in a careless or fiercely argumentative way'.[17] Indeed, in Tract 81 Pusey provides a particularly vivid demonstration of the contemporary currency of Newman's descriptions of the Alexandrian Church by speaking of the '*disciplina arcani* of the Anglican Church'.[18] *Arians* is, therefore, much more than a work of Church history.

4.2 Reserve in Arians

In *Arians* Newman presents reserve as something desirable and even necessary for Christian life. This goes back to the Caroline impulse to connect reserve with the 'pious sentiment' displayed in acknowledging the sanctity of the divine through

---

13. *Tracts*, p. 71.
14. Rowan Williams in the introduction to John Henry Newman, *Arians of the Fourth Century* (Leominster: Gracewing, 2001), p. 47.
15. Stephen Thomas, *Newman and Heresy: The Anglican Years* (Cambridge: Cambridge University Press, 1991), p. 3.
16. John Henry Newman, *Arians of the fourth century, their doctrine, temper, and conduct, chiefly as exhibited in the Councils of the Church, between A.D. 325, & A.D. 381* (London: E. Lumley, 1871), pp. 6–7.
17. Ibid., pp. 136–7. He also uses platitudes which are clearly wide-ranging, for example, 'those who attempt to speak at all times the naked truth' are certain to mislead those who are unable to understand, p. 137.
18. *Tracts*, p. 81.

a careful use of language. Arianism's heterodoxy is presented by Newman as rooted in an intemperate and immoderate use of language. He thus critiques a 'heretical spirit' with which this teaching emerged from Sophism.[19] He does not mean so much the content of writings such as those by Protagoras or Prodicus et al., but rather sophist techniques of rhetoric by which he claims the forerunners of Arianism were trained. Newman mentions Paulus of Samosata as a sophist who brought to the Church the 'use of those disputations and sceptical inquiries' which 'belonged to the Academy and other heathen philosophies'.[20] Rhetorical disputations are treated by Newman with great suspicion. He quotes Hooker as having written that the mind 'feeling present joy' in the things of God 'is always marvellously unwilling to admit any other cogitation, and in that case, casteth off those disputes whereunto the intellectual part at other times easily draweth'. To be drawn into rhetorical disputations is considered symptomatic of a cold or proud disposition, of being unmoved by the things of God and so subjecting them to outspoken critique. With reference to the disciples who consider Jesus to have spoken a 'hard saying' in John 6, Hooker says, 'because they enjoyed not' they 'disputed', but those who accepted the words of Christ 'disputed not, because they enjoyed'.[21]

Newman claims that Arianism's sophist roots explain its 'disputatious character'. Yet one might respond that surely there can be faithful and appropriately sensitive intellectual disputes about the faith, and that surely Newman himself would apply such behaviour to St Athanasius and other champions of orthodoxy during the Arius dispute. While this is of course correct, Newman's comments on the sophistical roots of Arianism are not merely ambivalent to rhetorical disputations but overtly negative in principle. The main issue with sophists is that they seek to ground faith in rational understanding and not vice versa. He gives an example of Bishop Arius' views being 'founded on a syllogism',[22] which is the inevitable result of having 'a sceptical rather than a dogmatic' basis.[23] To accept something as 'dogma', in faith, reflects the disposition Hooker connects with those disciples who held firm to Christ when he said 'lest you eat me'. That is, they were what he terms 'free' and 'unsuspicious' at what was revealed.[24]

This dogmatic or faithful disposition involves reserve, particularly in its contrast from the rhetorical style of intellectual disputations of the sophists, for it means quiet resignation and wordless devotion rather than subjecting things to intellectual critique. Newman says the sophists would go so far as to dispute merely 'for the sake of exercise or argument', in order to develop rhetorical skill regardless of the position being expressed. Then, the 'rhetoricians of Christian

---

19. Newman, *Arians*, p. 139.
20. Ibid., p. 3.
21. Ibid., pp. 18–19, quoting *Lawes of Ecclesiasticall Politie* v. 67.
22. Ibid., p. 28.
23. Ibid., pp. 26–7.
24. Ibid., pp. 36–7.

times introduced the same error into their treatment of the highest and most sacred subjects of theology'.²⁵ Having what we might today term a faulty grasp of fundamental theology around the primacy of faith over reason when it comes to revealed truth is thus connected by Newman to the careless and insensitive use of language. The 'highest and most sacred subjects' are never to be dragged into merely rhetorical display.

Elsewhere in *Arians* there are more indications that Newman considers reserve central to the Christian life on theological grounds. When he goes on to discuss further those 'disputants' with sophistical training, he criticizes also their recourse to worldly disciplines to try and make sense of divine mysteries. He writes, 'there are truths foreign to the province of the most exercised intellect' being 'received on the sole authority of Revelation'. Yet, faced with, say, 'the incomprehensibility of the Divine Essence', says Newman, 'the minds of speculative men' were 'impatient' of their 'ignorance' and rather than accept the inability of language to give voice to the divine mysteries they would use 'canons grounded on physics' as 'the basis for discussions about the possibilities and impossibilities in a spiritual substance' so they could continue to discourse 'confidently' and 'fallaciously'.²⁶

As for the *disciplina arcani* itself, Newman associates this particularly with the evangelizing mission of the Alexandrian Church, of whom he says 'proselytism' was a 'particular function'. He maintains that Alexandrian initiates separated exoteric from esoteric teachings, and when operating publicly or exoterically would therefore 'write, not with the openness of Christian familiarity, but with the tenderness or the reserve with which we are accustomed to address those who do not sympathize with us, or whom we fear to mislead or to prejudice against the truth, by precipitate disclosures of its details'.²⁷ This meant keeping the description of 'higher evangelical truths' reserved from public discussion, on account of the solemnity and significance of that to which such descriptions would witness. Hence, the 'secret discipline': a practice of 'self-restraint and abstinence' which was 'practiced' 'in the publication of the most sacred doctrines of our religion'.²⁸

The *disciplina arcani* is one side of this purportedly Alexandrian approach. The other is what Newman refers to as a 'mode of arguing and teaching' called '*economical*' (original italics).²⁹ This means the prudent dispensing of particular truths which minds hitherto unfamiliar with the faith might be suitably equipped to conceive appropriately, and the acceptance of which would lead towards

---

25. Ibid., pp. 32–3.

26. Ibid., pp. 33–4. It is worth mentioning that one weakness of *Arians* is that Newman does not follow through his lengthy historical development of Arianism through sophism into his later descriptions of the Arian position itself – the orthodox and heterodox positions are not laid out in such a way that the latter exhibits these qualities. There are no examples of rhetorical technique, nor elements drawn from other disciplines, provided.

27. Ibid., p. 41.

28. Ibid., pp. 49–50.

29. Ibid., p. 58.

developing aptitudes which might better suit them for yet more lofty reserved teachings. This is not about intellectual ability or mere 'education' as such but about the cultivation of a suitable affective and moral disposition for the full disclosure of the faith which should eventually follow. The Alexandrian approach is thus seen as both 'withholding the truth' and 'setting it out to advantage' in such a way so as to make due 'accommodation to the feelings and prejudices of the hearer'.[30] These included, particularly, 'moral truths', and the necessity of obedience, with a view to rousing 'the moral powers to internal voluntary action'.[31]

It is important to state, however, that Newman presents reserve towards discussing sacred things as much more than an evangelical technique, or as something that applies only to ante-Nicene Alexandria and the Church of England of the early 1830s. This can be seen in a discussion of what Newman terms 'the Allegorical Method'. He describes this as 'a mode of speaking', namely, 'the practice of generalizing facts into principles, of adumbrating greater truths under the image of lesser, of implying the consequences of the basis of doctrines in their correlatives, and altogether those instances of thinking, reasoning, and teaching, which depend on the use of propositions which are abstruse, and of connexions which are obscure'.[32] This dense description points to a creative mode of expression which might loosely be termed 'poetic'. This includes discerning matters of broad spiritual or moral import on the basis of individual facts and expressing them as principles; using particular illustrative examples to display highly significant realities (such as the 'higher evangelical truths') without spelling those realities out in language; and choosing to avoid exposing, say, the doctrines of the Trinity or Incarnation to inappropriately sceptical or rationalizing critique, opting rather to let those doctrines be alluded to through resonances, suggestion, synonyms, metaphors, and so on.

Allegorizing is thus for Newman something intrinsic to the interplay of language and Christian truth. He writes, 'When the mind is occupied by some vast and awful subject of contemplation, it is prompted to give utterance to its feelings in a figurative style; for ordinary words will not convey the admiration, nor literal words the reverence which possess it.'[33] This is connected to reserve firstly through a caution about 'ordinary' and 'literal words' being insufficient for divine things, and secondly, in the fact Newman maintains that traditions of typification follow from this allegorizing, thus providing safe images for subsequent generations to 'adopt' without 'fear of using unsanctioned language on a sacred subject'.[34] Such traditions are found even in Scripture itself, we read, the 'protest' of which 'against all careless expositions of its meaning, is strikingly implied in the extreme reserve and caution' with 'which it unfolds its own typical signification'.[35] Typology itself

30. Ibid.
31. Ibid., p. 49.
32. Ibid., p. 56.
33. Ibid., pp. 57–8.
34. Ibid., p. 58.
35. Ibid.

is thus for Newman a form of reserve, in which figurative motifs and images offer discrete means to convey profound truths in a way that philosophical assertions cannot, and which are uniquely able both to withhold truth from some while 'setting it out to advantage' to others.

Newman's Tractarian reserve applies even to Scripture, then. When it comes to Tradition, or more specifically Dogma, Newman adopts a position towards dogmatic formulations which shares the same commitment. In this connection we find some of the most well-known passages of *Arians*, where Newman presents the Church as having been better off when it had not dogmatically enunciated the higher evangelical truths. This is seen when Newman comes to discuss the Nicene Creed itself. He points out that 'the Object of religious veneration' is 'unseen, and dissimilar from all that is seen'. The 'Object' in this case is the Triune God, which, he goes on, 'reason can but represent ... in the medium of those ideas which the experience of life affords'. Then, 'the systematic doctrine of the Trinity may be conceived as the shadow, projected for the contemplation of the intellect, of the Object of scripturally-informed piety: a representation, economical, necessarily imperfect, as being exhibited in a foreign medium, and therefore including apparent inconstancies or mysteries'.[36]

Now, typology, allegorizing, and so on must also be considered representations 'in the medium' which 'the experience of life affords', but in their case the media are imagistic, imaginative, or poetic, and not 'projected for the contemplation of the intellect' alone so much as for piety. But they are for Newman superior on precisely this ground: 'The intellectual representation should ever be subordinate to the cultivation of religious affections.' He goes on, 'the inquisitiveness of a pious mind rests' when 'it has pursued the subject into the mystery which is its limit'. Arius disrupted and rudely awakened the restful contemplation of the Church into having to adopt the medium of explicit language to argue against erroneous disputations. Nicene dogma's 'presence became necessary to expel an usurping idol from the house of God'.[37]

Dogma in *Arians* is not therefore a cause for celebration or a triumphant achievement of the Holy Spirit working through the Church but something needed to dispel heresy. He goes further than this, however, in holding the arriving at dogmatic formulations itself to be unfortunate; not quite a necessary evil but still an occasion for sadness and mourning. He argues that the Church was at a great advantage before it had arrived at the systematic doctrine of the Trinity as a formal article of belief, before the Nicene Creed became incumbent on all the faithful and thus available for public display and scrutiny. He states, 'I avow my belief, that freedom from symbols and articles is abstractedly the highest state

---

36. Ibid., p. 143.

37. Ibid. The superiority of affections over words is a position Newman had held for some years, as is indicated by comments in a letter to Blanco White from 1828 which reads: 'words are not feelings' and 'intellect seems to be but the attendant and servant of right moral feeling', Newman, *Letters and Diaries I*, p. 60.

of Christian communion, and the peculiar privilege of the primitive Church.' He gives two reasons. In the first place, once language is unleashed on divine truths in an unrestrained fashion 'technicality and formalism' are the 'inevitable results of public confessions of the faith'. That is, when all are able to comment on sacred things, the precise formulation has to be as technically and formally watertight as possible to represent 'the Object' as well as it can – for pious sentiments can no longer be assumed. Secondly, because when these teachings are reserved, the affections can be suitably cultivated by proper training before the confessions are exposed to human scrutiny. Thus can profanation and wilful disbelief be avoided. He writes, 'the mysteries of divine truth' are then 'kept hidden in the bosom of the Church' and 'reserved by a private teaching',[38] so divine things are assured of being treated with 'pious sensitiveness' by the members of the Church, in the time of that 'free and unsuspicious teaching with which her childhood was blessed'.[39]

4.3 Difficulties with Arians

Along with the marked centrality of reserve for all dimensions of the Christian life in *Arians*, there are significant tensions at play. In the first place, there is a tension between his grounding of the importance of reserve in the Alexandrian Church, and his view that the primitive Church is the 'highest state of Christian communion'. That is, this reserve of sacred things, by Newman's own description, was included in a scheme of development and formation which the faithful hearer was meant to progress beyond. Newman connects the *disciplina arcani* with the Alexandrian Church, which, he states, was known for its 'diligent and systematic preparation of candidates for baptism'.[40] He argues that 'before reception into … full discipleship', there was a two- to three-year period of instruction in order that catechumens might 'try their obedience' and be prepared for 'revealed truth', that is, the 'peculiar doctrines of the Gospel', or the secret 'mysteries'. He refers here to both Hebrews and Corinthians, seeing so-called 'exoteric', or public teachings, as milk – and full-blown Trinitarian dogma as 'the strong meat of the Gospel'.[41]

Those Scriptural texts Newman takes for his sources urge believers to develop beyond the need for what Newman calls 'the most sacred Christian verities' to be reserved from them. The Corinthians are admonished for not being ready and for still being too worldly, which is shown by their quarrelling and jealousy.[42] Similarly, the Hebrews are admonished for being 'unskilled in the word of righteousness' and needing to 'go on toward perfection'.[43] Newman would argue that the Alexandrian

38. Ibid., pp. 36–7.
39. Ibid., pp. 135–6.
40. Ibid., p. 41.
41. Ibid.
42. Ibid., cf. Cor. 3.2-3.
43. Ibid., cf. Heb. 5.6-12.

pattern of formation was precisely that which would ensure that believers were suitably 'skilled' in righteousness, but the fact remains that, for many, dogmatic formulations are viewed far more positively than mere unfortunate necessities, rather as inextricable from doxology and as a crucial kataphatic counterpoint to apophatic impulses.

A second difficulty arises in that, if the Nicene Creed is merely an imperfect shadow, why is it binding on all Christians? This goes back to the raison d'être of *Arians*, wanting to establish how the Creeds and Councils of the primitive Church are binding on Anglicans while later Creeds and Councils are not. In an appendix of the book, Newman discusses the development of the terms *ousia* and *hypostasis* in a way which suggests their imperfection and limitedness as words is tempered and complemented by developments in their meanings and applications. He says, 'even in secular sciences, inaccuracy of thought and language is but gradually corrected' and 'in proportion as their subject matter is thoroughly scrutinized and mastered by the co-operation of many independent intellects, successfully engaged upon it'.[44] Rather than maintain that such secular developments in language do not apply to 'higher evangelical truths', he says, 'much more will this be the case, when we are concerned with subject-matters, of which, in our present state, we cannot possibly form any complete or consistent conception, such as the Catholic doctrines of the Trinity and Incarnation'. Their being 'above our intellectual reach' does not just preclude the use of the language, it alters language itself: 'They required new words, or words used in new senses, for their due enunciation.'

This nod towards language itself developing brings the driving problem of *Arians* back into view. Newman writes that 'new words' or 'words used in new sense' were 'not definitely supplied by Scripture or by tradition, nor for centuries by ecclesiastical authority, variety in the use, and confusion in the apprehension of them, were unavoidable in the interval'.[45] The problem with this statement, however, is that particular formulations are still clearly said to rest with ecclesiastical authority. In other words, Newman seems to have to rely on a position like that of Petavius. Either certain language itself has merit after all, and all language need not be subjected to reserve with the same intensity, *or* the difficulties with all language mean only authority can decide which formulations are the least unrepresentative of God, and which language therefore does not need to be reserved for its ecclesiastical sanction.

4.4 Summary

This chapter demonstrates that Newman's Tractarian theology shares the affection for reserve commonly associated with the English sensibility, and indeed this affection in Newman means reserve is elevated to a remarkably significant status

---

44. Ibid., p. 432.
45. Ibid.

for Christian life. Newman's rationales for allegory, typology, mission, catechesis, and even dogma are all grounded on the necessity of reserve in relation to the divine. At the same time, however, the combination of these rationales presents difficulties, insofar as Newman's admiration of Alexandrian catechesis and the *disciplina arcani* does not comfortably align with his acutely reserved attitude to dogmatic formulations, particularly as regards the relationship of dogma to doxology, and also *Arians*' modus operandi of avoiding recourse to ecclesiastical authority as the gatekeeper of authenticity. As it stands, then, Newman seems to be caught up in Englishness somewhat uncritically when it comes to reserve. He brings an attribute of the English sensibility into the very centre of Christian life, even to the point that other aspects of that life – such as *kataphasis* and doxology – are undermined to a degree that threatens to negate the argument of the book itself.

Chapter 5

NEWMAN'S TRACTARIAN EMPIRICISM

As with the connections shown in the previous chapter between compromise and reserve, empiricism cannot be separated from either. Links between empiricism and reserve are perceptible in *Arians*, where there is an empirical sentiment in Newman's commitment to the primacy of practical action against ideas.[1] Newman's critiques of the roots of Arianism in scepticism and rhetoric are linked with a working against obedience to Christian teaching, for he speaks of sophistical techniques doing 'mischief' to 'the simplicity of Christian morals',[2] with 'morals' here meaning the actual *doing* of what is commanded rather than disputing about the meaning of the commands. Secondly, the references to obedience in *Arians* show that it is practical action ('obedience to the moral law') that trains or forms a suitably reverent disposition in the believer.[3] In more general terms, there are self-evident links between empiricism and compromise, particularly in relation to 'common sense pragmatism', not to mention the relation between leaving the space between extremes indeterminate having great advantage for the 'generous simplicity of our obedience'.[4] As with compromise and reserve, moreover, Newman's empiricism has roots in the Caroline Divines. Part of the work of these Divines was 'the facilitation of an emergent Anglican piety', which included 'applying Christian

---

1. In a letter to Francis Newman from 1830, John Henry says on the question of assessing who is genuinely Christian and who is not: 'I give no credit to *words*' for 'my goal of sure hope as to another's spiritual state is the sight of a consistent *life*' (original italics), John Henry Newman, *The Letters and Diaries of John Henry Newman: Volume II: Tutor of Oriel, January 1827 to December 1831*, edited by I. Ker and T. Gornall (Oxford: Clarendon Press, 1979), p. 183.

2. Newman, *Arians*, p. 32.

3. This is one of the main things Newman claims the Alexandrians imparted with their 'exoteric' teaching. Moreover, he applies the disclosive power of obedience to present-day believers, writing on how his contemporaries 'publicly canvass the most solemn truths' when 'it is as useless as it is unseemly to discuss [these truths] in public' because they are 'attainable' by 'slow degrees' and 'with strict obedience to the light which has already been granted'. Ibid., pp. 135–6.

4. Newman, *Prophetical Office*, p. 104.

devotion to daily discipleship'.[5] This was to offset the Reformers' strict faith-works dichotomy with the cultivation of an obedience which is typically considered more prominent in what they would term 'Roman' theology.

5.1 Action over idea in the Parochial and Plain Sermons

In the *Parochial and Plain Sermons*, delivered at St Mary's and published in seven volumes between 1834 and 1843, obedience emerges as the primary theme of the entire collection numbering some 173 individual sermons. A collection of this length cannot be explored exhaustively here, but the salient aspects of what Newman claims about obedience can be outlined in order to show how it is that action is primary over idea in his preaching. Indeed, the sermons provide one of the first examples of what Just called Newman's 'lifelong orientation' to 'the individual and the concrete, to facts and "particulars"'.[6]

Firstly, Newman maintains that obedience is necessary because it abnegates self-centeredness, it challenges self-will. He claims 'it is nothing to *know* what is right, unless we *do* it' (original emphasis), because knowledge itself will not challenge self-will, or rather, knowing the truth and not acting on it will leave one in the same state of life as one was in prior to gaining that knowledge. This is because 'the most difficult part' of the Christian life is 'to surrender' to God 'in deed and act'.[7] The implication is that while an intellectual acceptance of religious truth might be difficult, it is nothing compared to the surrender of one's self that action necessitates. To accept something as true is very different from placing oneself in service of that truth, letting the course of one's life be altered by it. What Newman means by obedience is 'particular definite acts' in daily life. He does not focus on works of piety like prayer or receiving the sacraments, so much as putting one's self at the service of others. He lists some examples of what one who sets out to do a 'little deed of obedience' might undertake: 'he denies some comfort to relieve the sick and needy, or curbs his temper, or forgives an enemy, or asks forgiveness for an offence committed by him, or resists the clamour or ridicule of the world'. By doing such things, the believer 'evinces more true faith than could be shown by the most fluent religious conversation, the most intimate knowledge of Scripture doctrine, or the most remarkable agitation and change of religious

---

5. Kenneth Stevenson, 'Caroline Divines', in *The Oxford Companion to Christian Thought*, edited by Adrian Hastings (Oxford: Oxford University Press, 2000), pp. 97–8; see also Phillips, 'Service in Perfect Freedom: The Precious Gift of the Caroline Divines', in *Anglican Patrimony in Catholic Community: The Gift of the Ordinariates*, edited by Tracey Rowland (London: T&T Clark, 2021), pp. 151–66.

6. Walter Jost, *Rhetorical Thought in John Henry Newman* (South Carolina: University of South Carolina Press, 1989), p. 2.

7. Newman, *Parochial and Plain Sermons*, pp. 22 and 112.

sentiments'.[8] If one converses fluently on theology, has a sound grasp of the Bible, or is even caught up in devotional fervour during prayer, one's life can still remain more or less exactly as it was without any of these things. It is a truism that 'the road to hell is paved with good intentions', and for Newman it is precisely the stage of 'intending' where faith tends to falter, for 'doing is at far greater distance from intending to do than you at first sight imagine'.[9]

Of course amending one's life through obedience is not for Newman an end in itself. It is the primary means by which a believer gives glory to God. Surrendering oneself to God in action and deed is 'the temper under which men obey' because of 'the humble and earnest desire to please Christ' which 'causes and attends on actual services'.[10] It is such 'practices of lowly obedience which alone can prove [believers] to be Christ's at the last day'.[11] According to these sermons, believers must practice an acute vigilance towards their own behaviour, not just in the sense of being ever-attentive for opportunities to obey but also exercising great care not to take rest in knowledge, to mistake knowledge of Christ as an end in itself. Newman goes so far as to point out that even the knowledge that 'knowledge is nothing' can itself surreptitiously and insidiously position itself as an alternative to obedience, diffusing the biting urgency of Christ's commands. Then, '*knowing* that knowledge is nothing' is 'made to be something', and 'we make it count, and thus we cheat ourselves'.[12]

While it is true Newman does not preach that obedience is an end in itself, it does bear what we might term 'secondary fruit' in the life of the believers. That is, he presents obedience as formative for Christian life, as indeed *Arians* presents obedience for the Alexandrian Church. Without the 'surrender' of the will that comes with 'action and deed', he says a religious system will simply grow on self-will. Believers who 'profess' religion without 'doing' it, he says, 'add it to what they *are*, they ingraft it upon the selfish and worldly habits of an unrenewed heart'. Obedience renews the heart, or rather allows Christ to renew the heart, otherwise one might form 'a system of morality and religion' of one's 'own'.[13] Unacted-upon knowledge of Christ is then simply 'ingrafted' on fallen self-will, giving a religious veneer to life without Christ conquering the heart. Moreover, as obedience fosters our interior regeneration by Christ, its neglect tends towards degeneration. Newman highlights that inaction precedes unbelief. Habitual avoidance or neglect of obedience enables self-will to reassert itself, eventually placing even the knowledge of Christ in jeopardy: 'doubts, if we have any, will be found to arise after *disobedience*'.[14] Obedience concretely brings people to God, inaction carries them away. Newman

8. Ibid., p. 112.
9. Ibid., p. 79.
10. Ibid., p. 112.
11. Ibid., p. 80.
12. Ibid., p. 22.
13. Ibid., pp. 24–5.
14. Ibid., p. 130.

says that 'if we but obey God strictly', before long, 'faith will become like sight'. Such sight is 'the blessedness of confirmed obedience' and this why the statement 'deeds, not words and wishes', he claims, 'must be the watchword of your warfare and the ground of your assurance'.[15]

Why is it that Newman gives such significance to practical action? In short, obedience calls for a surrender of internal security because the realm of action – the empirical present – is necessarily a realm of uncertainty, a domain in which knowledge alone does not hold sway. There is thus a profound analogy in the dynamics pertaining to life being lived in practical activity and life being lived in the presence of God. In both instances, truth transcends human capacities of knowing. Both faith and obedience are premised on what Newman describes elsewhere as 'the indefinite range of God's operations beyond our means of apprehending them'.[16]

This can be described using Newman's examples of obedient action. One can think firstly in terms of consequences. Depriving oneself of some comfort to relieve the sick and needy, for example, could result in the offering of a gift to another which is not well-received, or which inadvertently causes offence. Asking forgiveness for a past misdemeanour can backfire and place yet further strain on the relationship in question. This is not to mention all the uncertainty that attends self-examination of motives in the complexity of human life. Forgiving an enemy can show itself to have been mere lip service following an explosion of anger sometime after the event, or curbing one's temper can result in an unexpected eruption of repressed annoyance elsewhere. Doing good deeds can and does easily slip into the vanity of wanting others to see oneself as holy. Most significantly, knowing that 'your father who sees in secret will reward you' is of course never a demonstrable truth like other truths in the standard order of knowledge. Obedience renders oneself vulnerable in innumerable ways, and Christian obedience is undertaken on the promise of an unseen divine acknowledgement. Indeed, Newman writes that action issues from faith, and is therefore itself the opposite of doubt.[17] Weatherby has claimed that Newman's thinking is pessimistic and modern, because he accepts God's being beyond our means of apprehension in a way alien to the pre-Enlightenment English tradition of Hooker and the Carolines.[18] While Newman is certainly modern in this respect, he is hardly pessimistic. Rather he seeks to put God right at the centre of the more empirically focused post-Enlightenment mindset.

15. Ibid., pp. 110 and 130.
16. Tract 73.
17. Newman, *Parochial and Plain Sermons*, pp. 25–6.
18. Weatherby connects this also with the 'real apprehension' of the *Grammar*, discussed in Chapters 10 and 11 of this book, but there is no evidence that his recourse to the empirical present is in anyway a 'lament' for a harmony of the supernatural and natural which has been lost in modernity, as Weatherby contends. Weatherby, *Newman in His Age*, pp. 19–20.

Acting obediently is antithetical to what Newman calls in Tract 73 'rationalism'. He says that to rationalize 'is to ask for reasons out of place; to ask improperly how we are to *account* for certain things, and to be unwilling to believe them unless they can be accounted for'. Rationalism is then a 'denying' of 'the indefinite range of God's operations beyond our means of apprehending them'. Acting obediently in faith, by contrast, is to surrender to that 'indefinite range' in the complexity of life. This can be seen most fully when Newman describes 'Mystery' in the same Tract. Rationalism discards Mystery, we read, because it cannot countenance the 'notion of half views and partial knowledge, of guesses; surmises, hopes and fears, of truths firmly apprehended and not understood, of isolated facts in the great scheme of providence'. Embarking on a course of action by definition requires half views and partial knowledge, guesses, surmises, hopes and fears, and an overarching trust in God's providence. For this reason, Newman states in another sermon that that which 'brings us *practical* and *useful knowledge* about our souls' actually 'in *consequence of* doing so, brings us mysteries'. Practical and useful knowledge is knowledge focused on action in the empirical world, and this is something we 'gain', he says, 'at the price of intellectual perplexity'.[19]

It could be countered that the marked focus on obedience in the *Parochial and Plain Sermons* is a reflection of their homiletic character. Preaching is exhortation, and perhaps Newman focuses on exhorting his congregations to take action due to the medium under discussion. While there is some truth in this, it would be a disservice to downplay the theme of action in those sermons as a result. For the theme is present in the Tracts, where Tract 2 mentions that the Creedal statement about the Church is given 'as a *fact*, and a fact *to be believed*, and therefore practical' showing that belief and action cannot be separated. The impulse which would later in Tract 72 be applied to rationalism is described in Tract 8 as 'a cold spirit' which has 'crept into the Church', of 'demanding rigid demonstration for every religious practice and observance'. Those under the influence of this cold spirit are compared to the 'husbandman's son in the Gospel, who said "I go, sir – AND WENT NOT"'.[20]

In the *Lectures on Justification* Newman applies the *via media* method to post-Reformation debates on justification, claiming that 'the English divines' tread a middle path between the Scylla of Lutheranism and the Chabdis of Trent. He maintains a position whereby justification is 'vouchsafed to those who are moved by God's grace to claim it', that is, by faith, and that those believers are 'by the same grace ... moved to do their duty' by 'obedience'.[21] To discuss here exactly how Newman tiptoes between Luther and Trent would divert from present purposes, but suffice to say he makes great efforts to affirm the centrality of works as always inextricable from faith, even if formally or conceptually distinct. That is,

---

19. Newman, *Parochial and Plain Sermons*, p. 134.
20. *Tracts*, p. 50.
21. John Henry Newman, *Lectures on Justification* (London: Longmans, Green, 1892), p. 1.

justification is said to involve not only a 'nominal change' generating a 'nominal righteousness', a mere 'external blessing', but a blessing 'penetrating inwards into our heart and spirit, joints and marrow, pervading us with a real efficacy'.[22] Conceptually we can of course distinguish between faith and obedience, and indeed it may be necessary at times to do so if legalism or works righteousness threaten. But note, for Newman this distinction has no reality in life itself: 'One cannot be separated from the other except in idea.' The 'first blessing' of faith runs into the second blessing of obedience 'as its necessary limit' and if obedience is 'rejected', then faith is rejected too. Separating them is thus described as separating the sun's rays from the sun, or the 'power of purifying from fire and water'.[23]

5.2 Common sense pragmatism

The discussion thus far shows that the priority of action over idea is unquestionable in Newman's writing on the individual believer; when it comes to applying the corporate or collective application of the same principles, the situation is more ambiguous. The link between individual and collective emphases on empirical action can be seen in Pusey. Having fully aligned himself with the Tractarians in 1835, Pusey's first contribution to their flagship texts was a lengthy Tract on the practice of fasting which had long since been neglected in the Church of England. Having discussed the scriptural bases for the practice, and discerned it is not incumbent on all the faithful yet also promisingly advantageous to some, Pusey makes passing reference to broadly Burkean principles which give a good example of how prioritizing action over idea has corporate and collective purchase. He writes, 'in practical matters, the great test of the expediency of any habit, for which we have not direct divine authority, is *experience*'. That is, experience is the great test of how beneficial something may be, for merely assessing the *concept* of fasting is to be stuck in 'abstract reasonings about the possibilities or tendencies of things'. In moral matters, though, we are as sick persons under the influence of self-will and concupiscence, and similarly he says we would not 'hasten' to help 'sick men' with 'abstract reasonings'. Ever the outlier when it comes to Tractarian antipathy about what they termed 'Germanism', Pusey quotes Goethe: 'People … need a succession of the like actions whereby a habit may be formed.'[24] For Edmund Burke, the collective habits of a people cement into custom. Herein lies the link with the English tradition of common law, establishing norms gradually through experience, through practice, not through artificial and abstract impetuses or 'radical blueprints'.

Returning to Newman, the basic pattern of common law is something he connects with Tradition in theology. He uses the analogy to explain 'Romanism'

---

22. Ibid., p. 34.
23. Ibid., p. 154.
24. *Tracts*, p. 143 n.24.

to his readers in the *Prophetical Office*. He says that 'Romanists' include under the category of Tradition 'the whole system of faith and ordinances which they have received from the generation before them'. He assumes his readers should be familiar with this notion, insofar as 'we all go by Tradition in matters of this world'. After all, 'at this very time great part of the law of the land is administered under the sanction of such a Tradition; it is not contained in any formal or authoritative code, it depends on custom or precedent'. Tradition in the Church is thus similarly 'uniform custom'. Romanists, of course, 'allege that there is his important difference between their custom and all other customs in this world', namely, that it can be traced back to the Apostles, and 'is in consequence of divine not human authority'. They therefore claim that it 'is true and intrinsically binding as well as expedient', which goes beyond the outcome of what Pusey connected with habit. Needless to say, the Tractarian Newman currently disagrees with Rome. He says Romanist Tradition 'stops short of the Apostles' and is actually 'an upstart Tradition'.[25]

His attitude to Roman Tradition comes as no surprise of course, but it is surprising that Newman both holds to the centrality of a developing Tradition in the Church, formed by habit and custom operating over time, while at the same time calling for radical innovation, for a 'second Reformation'. This is not to assume that Burkean understandings of tradition, nor common law, nor indeed the overarching commitment to empiricism as pragmatism cannot admit of any impulses to change. It is rather that change is understood to be attentive and receptive to real-world circumstances, working from the 'bottom-up' as it were, not imposing ideas on circumstances 'external' to whatever state of affairs is at stake. It is also understood as following certain 'laws', often connected by its proponents with patterns of organic development and growth, distinguishing it from impulses which are artificially imposed. Hence, Burke's aforementioned 'slow but well-sustained progress'. In this sense, a commitment to action over idea is mirrored on a corporate or collective level, working from practice to ideas and principles, modifying by way of discrete precedents invoked by specific circumstances. Indeed, to break with patterning in the name of a 'radical blueprint' like a 'second Reformation' threatens to present exactly what Newman says has become of Rome: 'an upstart Tradition'. That is, it breaks the chain of continuity going back to its source, with artificial and inauthentic doctrine leading it astray.

Now while the *via media* is not strictly speaking novel, as such, even the Tractarian Newman himself describes it as hitherto pertaining only to the realm of 'idea' and not the empirical reality of the Church. There is no pragmatism here, he is not working from existing states of affairs, but seeking to generate new states of affairs by bringing an *idea* to bear on the real world. He says the *via media* 'has never been realized' and is hitherto 'a mere system' and as such might be 'nothing better than an assemblage of words'.[26] Again, he is aware of the criticism, for he

---

25. Newman, *Prophetical Office*.
26. Ibid., p. 129.

acknowledges those who will maintain that it is right for 'English doctrine' not to be 'embodied in any substantive form'. To leave the *via media* as just ideas and words, however, would be to 'make reason the judge of it'.[27] The issue here is that it is precisely systems which appear neat and beneficial at the level of reason but have no purchase in real circumstances, which the empirical pragmatism of the English sensibility abjures. The common tradition of English life necessitates that to impose such ideas on reality tends to be at best futile, and at worst woefully disruptive.

Newman here clearly breaks with the pragmatic empiricism of someone like Richard Hooker, for whom a combination of insights drawn from 'nature, Scripture, and experience' gives the requisite material for a rationale of the authenticity of the 'English Church'.[28] As Weatherby points out, Hooker's theological reasoning is based on a fundamental complementarity between the revelation of Scripture and pragmatic experience in the world. He notes, the harmony between God and reality was also hugely important for Hooker's successors, particularly John Donne, who 'absorbed Hooker's conception of the relationship between God and nature', which 'is closely related' to 'the *via media*'. This middle path is very different to Newman's, insofar as worldly reality (experience and nature) constitutes one pole, and Scripture another. This is said by Weatherby to evince a conviction that 'the established (worldly) order of things' is 'holy', underlying both Donne and Hooker.[29] But as put by James Cameron, the Anglican Church had not 'in practice' been the body which the Tractarian's 'own theological position' wanted it to be.[30]

5.3 Summary

This chapter demonstrates that while Newman's Tractarian theology broadly shares the empirical proclivities of the English sensibility in his prioritizing of action over idea in the *Parochial and Plain Sermons*, this is not the case as regards the *Prophetical Office*'s working against collective experience through common sense pragmatism when it comes to the *via media*. As it stands then, the Tractarian Newman has relatively balanced influence of empiricism into his theology, wholeheartedly encouraging it for the individual believer but challenging it when it comes to collective self-identity in Anglican ecclesiology.

On compromise Newman seemed to be caught up in an aspect of the English sensibility while also straining against it. On reserve Newman seemed to be so caught up in an aspect of the English sensibility that it threatens to become inconsistent with his theological aims. On empiricism it seems to be a balanced

---

27. Ibid., p. 22.
28. Weatherby, *Newman in His Age*, p. 14.
29. Ibid., p. 42.
30. Cameron in Newman, *Development*, p. 17.

application for different contexts. The following chapters will revisit each of these aspects in turn as they emerge in the writings from the Second Spring period which begins around the time of Newman's conversion and changes sometime before he writes the *Apologia*.

Chapter 6

COMPROMISE IN THE SECOND SPRING

Compromise in Newman's Tractarian period suggests he is caught up in Englishness while also straining against it. On the one hand, he gives a corollary of this element of Englishness, indeterminateness, theological authority insofar as it avoids legalism and safeguards mystery. On the other hand, he determines the parameters of his discussion to a degree that threatens inconsistency. He does this, moreover, acknowledging that there are dangers with confusing national sentiment for religion, reducing it 'to mere literature'.[1] The Tractarian Newman is thus at odds with himself in this regard, and in this chapter we shall see this tension reach dramatic levels of intensity. Indeed, Newman's relationship to the *via media* is a defining element of the defining moment of his life, his conversion in 1845. His forsaking of the *via media* then characterizes much of his work during the Second Spring period, particularly its most fiery and polemical writings. One can go so far as to say Newman's change of position towards the *via media* exemplifies his own 'Second Spring': entering into youth (springtime) as a mature adult, beginning again as a foreigner under the auspices of the Catholic Church.

6.1 The event of 1841

By Newman's own reckoning, his struggle with the *via media* is the decisive factor in leading him to convert.[2] He highlights a realization that came to him while translating the treatises of St Athanasius in 1841 as one supremely important moment above all others. This is famously described in the *Apologia* (1864), but my discussion in this chapter stays focused on Newman's immediate post-conversion period, and therefore concentrates on the less well-known description of that moment in *Difficulties* (1850). One of the contentions of this book is that there are significant changes in Newman's relationship with the English sensibility around the time of the *Apologia*, and taking each of his accounts independently helps make this case, as we shall see when studying the *Apologia* in Chapter 9.

---

1. Newman, *Prophetical Office*, p. 22.
2. Ker, *Newman*, pp. 257–315.

Newman's dramatic volte-face away from the *via media* occurred as his translating of St Athanasius in 1841 led him to revisit the Arian controversy. He recounts these studies in *Difficulties* to give an example to his Anglican audience of how the witness of the Church Fathers can lead someone to Rome. It is a counterargument to a defining supposition of the Tractarians (whom he now calls 'the movement of 1833') that Antiquity speaks against Rome. The crucial realization is preceded, we read, by a foreshadowing in the summer of 1839, when Newman undertook a reading of the Fathers focused on the Monophysite controversy. He says that 'at once and irrevocably I found my faith in the tenableness of the fundamental principle of Anglicanism disappear, and a doubt of it implanted in my mind which was never eradicated'.[3] This 'fundamental principle' is of course the *via media*. He goes on to say that in 1841 he 'clearly saw' the 'same phenomenon that had startled me' in the Monophysite controversy applied also to the Arian. This phenomenon is that the *via media* is not a 'novelty in ancient history' and has 'a series of prototypes'.[4] Later he describes 'three parties on the historical scene' of the Arian controversy, one of which is the prototype of the ecclesiology of the *via media* compromise. Firstly, 'the See and Communion of Rome', or the orthodox, secondly, the 'pure Protestant', or the heterodox Arians, and thirdly, 'a cautious middle party' which sought to mediate between the first and second parties and avoid both extremes.[5]

For Newman simply to have decided Rome was right after all would not, for the Tractarian Newman, have equated to orthodoxy. He was hardly inclined to Rome when he commenced his readings of the Fathers. The transformative factor in Newman's thinking is centred on a change in his understanding of truth in relation to dogma. From this change he discerns that Rome teaches the dogmatic truth, and that any compromise with that truth constitutes untruth. We have seen that in the *Prophetical Office* Newman approaches truth as if it were an Aristotelian virtue which lies in between extremes. Aristotle himself does not have such a virtue in the *Nicomachean Ethics*,[6] although he does have a virtue of truthfulness (ἀληθεύειν) for which the extremes are either boastfulness or understatement of one's accomplishments. In fact, one can suggest truth can never be a virtue as a mean, as such, for the simple reason that, when viewing certain objective facts the state of affairs in question is *either* true or false. The most obvious example is truths of basic arithmetic. There is no middle path between 2+2 = 4 or 5, there is no excess of deficiency of truth between one party holding that 2+2 = 5 and another that it equals 50.

The primary change in Newman's thinking is the recognition that a truth of dogma partakes of a similarly sharp binary between either truth or falsity.

---

3. Newman, *Difficulties*, pp. 372–3.
4. Ibid., p. 37.
5. Ibid., p. 378.
6. See H. J. Curzer, *Aristotle and the Virtues* (Oxford: Oxford University Press, 2012), pp. 195–220.

6. Compromise in the Second Spring

This derails Anglican attempts to apply the Lérinian dictum. If it is true for the Monophysite and Arian controversies, it must also be the case for Trent. Then the compromise formulae of Anglicanism are either true or false as well: there is then no sanction for a *via media* between Trent and Wittenberg, Rome and Geneva, nor what Newman calls 'Romanism' and 'popular Protestantism' in England. Hence, Newman comes to hold that 'the *via media* is nothing else than Protestant', by which he means that it is untrue to say 2 plus 2 equalling 20 being more true than it equalling 40, because 20 is the middle position between 4 and 40.[7] Not 'to submit to the Church is to oppose her', he writes, 'for medium there is none'.[8]

There is therefore no longer any place in Newman's thinking for a position like that of Mr Vincent in the novel *Loss and Gain* (1848) who 'had a great idea of the *via media* being the truth' but was 'always saying things and then unsaying them'.[9] The realization is central to an *Essay in the Development of Christian Doctrine* (1845). It is particularly perceptible in the example Newman gives of his second test of authenticity for a doctrinal development, 'Continuity of Principles'.[10] This is presented as a means by which, in seeking to discern the authenticity of a doctrinal development, that development is scrutinized as to whether or not the basic principles of Christian doctrine are continuous before and with the development itself. He maintains that 'the destruction of the special laws or principles of a development is its corruption'.[11] Saliently for present purposes, the example of 'Continuity of Principle' Newman provides in the *Development* essay is that truth is 'one, unalterable, consistent, imperative, and saving'.[12] He says this, specifically, is the 'cardinal distinction between Christianity and the religions and philosophies by which it was surrounded'.[13] He also calls the continuous principle 'the Dogmatic Principle', which is that 'there is a truth' and 'there is one truth'. With 'the old established paganism' and Christianity in Antiquity, he claims, two 'opinions' encountered each other, and while both may be 'abstractedly true', only one is 'a matter of life and death'.[14] Unlike Mr Vincent in *Loss and Gain*, the early faithful were not 'always saying things and then unsaying them', the early Church 'could not call evil good and good evil'.[15] For 'contradictions could not both be real; when an affirmative was true, a negative was false'.[16]

---

7. Newman, *Difficulties*, p. 377.
8. Ibid.
9. John Henry Newman, *Loss & Gain* (Leominster: Gracewing, 2014), pp. 74–5.
10. Newman, *Development*, pp. 124–6, see Chapter 1 n.1 for change from 'continuity' to 'unity' in the 1878 edition.
11. Ibid., p. 126.
12. Ibid., p. 352.
13. Ibid. Newman includes Judaism among these religions, strangely.
14. Ibid., p. 357.
15. Ibid., p. 358.
16. Newman, *Loss and Gain*, p. 34. Newman's change in understanding how truth applies to dogma is further indicated by his use of analogies with mathematics to describe the

The significance of this change for the argument of this book is indicated by the fact Newman presents the second test as directly leading into the third, 'the Power of Assimilation'. He writes, 'Christianity has from first to last kept fixed principles in view in the course of its developments, and *thereby* has been able to incorporate doctrine which was external to it without losing its own.'[17] This points us forward towards understanding how it is Newman moves towards displaying something like the assimilative power of Catholicism as operative in nineteenth-century England, but such displays are not yet prevalent. Rather, the tone is now confrontational, and the emphasis is on how continuity of principle, or the 'dogmatic principle', collides with opposing world views. In the 'collision' with paganism, we read, Christianity 'broke into pieces its antagonists, and divided the spoils'.[18]

Some readers will be wondering whether Newman would accept that there are states of affairs for which the dogmatic approach to truth does not apply. Surely some circumstances require that truth is approached as a mean between extremes, not least when seeking consensus in the civic order and other social interrelations. Then the principle of compromise of course comes into its own as the means by which differing parties can cooperate peacefully and constructively. The answer is that Newman does of course accept this, and he returns to this distinction on various occasions in his writings. During his Tractarian writings he had already argued that Catholic Tradition functioned like English Common Law in many respects except for the fact it understands itself as 'not only expedient but true'. The distinction is thus one between what Newman calls 'truth and expedience'. After 1841 he decides that Anglicanism mistakes expedience for truth, and thereby opts to compromise even with God himself. This is shown by his disparaging remarks about Bishop Warburton (1698–1779) in *Difficulties*, who stated clearly that 'public utility and truth coincide', and that such utility is 'a sure rule and measure of truth'.[19] Warburton also writes that 'wherever opinions clash with civil peace, those opinions ... are either no truth, or truths of no importance'.[20]

With this in mind we can understand why, in his description of the 1841 realization, he says the idea of truth as a mean 'will find especial acceptance with the civil magistrate' who will welcome 'joyfully' some 'form of theology, whose very mission it is to soften the violence of polemics' and 'to soften and accommodate difference'.[21] The realization at stake, then, is the moment he reverses his refusal to accept that Catholic doctrine is not only expedient, which any tradition must be

---

test of 'Continuity of Principle'. He writes, 'in mathematic creations figures are formed on distinct formulae, which are the laws under which they are developed'. *Development*, p. 124.

17. Newman, *Development*, p. 352 (my emphasis).
18. Ibid., p. 358.
19. Quoted by Newman in *Difficulties*, p. 190, see note 2.
20. Newman, *Difficulties*, p. 193.
21. Ibid., p. 375.

in order to endure for any length of time, but also true, guaranteeing its endurance for all eternity.

While Newman leaves us in little doubt as to the importance of the event of 1841 as the site of his realization, it is common for secondary commentators to describe this event purely in terms of recognizing a pattern in history and then applying that to Anglicanism in his own day. This is of course partially correct, but it neglects that the substantive change beneath this moment, or resulting from it, is essentially a theological shift: the recognition of the dogmatic principle pertaining exclusively to Catholicism, which, if altered (as in sixteenth- and seventeenth-century Anglicanism and later Tractarianism), constitutes a corruption as grievous as either of the extremes proponents of the *via media* seek to avoid. When Newman says that most oft-quoted statement, 'Rome was where it is now', this does not mean just that the Son is eternally begotten of the Father before all ages, or that Rome occupied the orthodox position, but that that orthodox position was grounded on a continuity of principle which must *by definition* apply to Rome in the 1840s and indeed for all time.

6.2 Against Englishness

6.2.1 Against the Englishness of the via media

Save for a few remarks in the *Prophetical Office* and some of the *Tracts*, the Englishness of the *via media* as a supreme example of compromise is barely mentioned in Newman's Tractarian writings. This changes dramatically for Newman during his Second Spring period. Now he repeatedly draws attention to the *via media* not only as emblematic of the English sensibility but also to this exemplary character as its fatal weakness in the collision with Catholic dogma. This begins in *Loss and Gain*, the first work published after his conversion. Mr Vincent is Newman's representation of an Anglican who holds firm to the *via media*, and also of the typical Englishman. Mr Vincent's reasoning in favour of consistent compromise, interestingly, is that it portrays a certain English superiority in that enquirers into Christianity do not have everything laid out for them, but must use their own discretion to find the mean between Christianity's continental variants. Mr Vincent thus describes the 'depth and power' and the 'fullness' of the Caroline Divines as 'English', because they display 'that robust, masculine, noble independence' of 'the English mind' which is like 'a tree rich in foliage … no sickenly denizen of the hothouse, or helpless dependent of the garden wall'.[22] Moreover, the dramatic climax of the novel involves a Catholic priest entering the scene towards the end of the novel, whom Sheridan Gilley suggests should be understood as Newman himself. The main protagonist Mr Reding mistakes the priest as foreign – indeed, as a Frenchman – and even tries to start a conversation with him in French, being startled when the priest answers in native English. Mr

---

22. Newman, *Loss & Gain*, pp. 84–5.

Reding describes those like Mr Vincent as belonging to a 'set' of 'well-informed and excellent men' who cannot appreciate Catholicism 'on the excuse' that there are 'arguments on both sides'. The English priest in French garb replies that 'it is not one set of men', but that this is 'the grievous deficiency of Englishmen altogether'.[23]

Mr Vincent's praising of the 'robust, masculine, noble independence' of the 'English mind' as displayed by the compromise settlement of the *via media* hints towards why Newman connects compromise with the ideal type of a 'free born Englishman'. In *Difficulties*, he claims the Anglican formularies 'are but the expression of national sentiment', because 'the free-born, self-dependent, animal mind of the Englishman' is exemplified by the measure of free discretion they necessitate from their adherents. He asks if it is not 'to obtrude the mysteries' of a 'dogmatic' religion if they are forced 'upon a nation which intimately feels that each individual is to be its own judge'.[24] He later comments that the real reason behind Anglicans 'extolling the Episcopate and the Prayer Book' is mere 'expedience'.[25] The *Present Position* (1851) presents the *via media* as exemplary of the English sensibility even more forcefully. His primary concern in these lectures is to discern why 'in this intelligent nation, and in this rational nineteenth century, we Catholics are so despised and hated by our countrymen'. He argues that this reflects English self-understanding of themselves as 'a free people', who are so free they dare to insist that Catholicism and Protestantism are 'both right and wrong' and that there are 'two truths'.[26] He makes frequent reference to what he calls 'the Englishman's maxim', *audi alteram partem*. Yet, when it comes to Catholicism, this same noble and freeborn specimen 'has intractable prejudices, and resolutely repudiates any view but that which is familiar to him from his childhood'.[27]

Present Position's seventh lecture on 'assumed principles' on the Protestant world view is highly praised by theologians. Here, Newman describes the phenomenon of what Reding had called 'well-informed and excellent men' deciding to study some Catholic theology, presumably to put in action their all-important maxim of *audi alteram partem*. He says that 'they take up one of our books', but 'alas they are flung back at once', for 'they see so much which they cannot abide at all'. The reason for this is, put simply, that Catholic teaching cannot accommodate half-truths: they 'had hoped to find some middle term', but could not, because the 'fundamental principles' of Catholicism are radically different to the 'moral identity' of the well-meaning Englishman.[28] In discussing how to understand such fundamental principles in the formation of what we now term 'world views', we encounter the passage previously quoted in Chapter 2 as an example of Newman's belief in the importance of locality rather than race in forming cultural

23. Ibid., p. 377.
24. Newman, *Difficulties*, pp. 19 and 24.
25. Ibid., p. 137.
26. Newman, *Present Position*, pp. 1, 2, 5.
27. Ibid., p. 24.
28. Ibid., pp. 272–3.

sensibilities. He states that certain principles 'are common to extended localities', and people are thus imbibed with them by the culture and sensibility of the place in which they were born. Hence, 'nations have very frequently one and the same set of First Principles', and the fundamental conviction of the English, the moral identity of the Englishman, is to find the 'middle term'. It is these, he says, 'who feel themselves superior to the multitude' because they can 'like' each thing 'for what is good in it, though they may not follow it themselves'.[29] Like the Very Reverend Dr Brownside in *Loss and Gain*, they consider 'revealed dogmas' to be 'neither good or bad in themselves' but rather 'national', for the Anglican formularies, he says in a sermon, are seen as '*our* mode of expressing enduring truths'.[30] The fault, *pace* the Englishman, comes if one were 'insisting on them', or rather, arguing that, when it comes to dogmatic truth, nuances about modes of expression are neither here nor there.[31] There is just a choice between truth and falsity, and the parameters of that choice are not set by the freeborn Englishman.

6.2.2 Against English 'viewiness'

We can now see that the Tractarian Newman defends English 'indeterminateness' in ways similar to the errors of the 'freeborn Englishman' he later derides. The *Prophetical Office* claims that allowing for personal discretion in Christian obedience is more noble and important than adhering to concrete stipulations, and that determination tends towards constructing 'systems' which inherently undermine God as mystery. On Christian obedience, Newman takes issue directly with himself in the *Development* essay. Here, he seeks to show why criticisms of Roman infallibility are wrong, and he argues against the previous discussion in the *Prophetical Office*, from which he quotes extensively. He characterizes his own position as holding that the Roman approach to infallibility 'would destroy our probation' by 'dissipating doubt, precluding the exercise of faith, and obliging us to obey whether we wish it or no'.[32] Unsurprisingly, he now concludes that the determinateness entailed that infallibility 'does not interfere with moral probation' after all.[33] His reasoning will perhaps give some solace to those who today have grave doubts about an overbearing dogmatism. After all, it is one thing to say dogmas involve objective truths like those of mathematics, but credal statements are not expressed with the singular referents of number and arithmetic and are thus open to conflicting interpretations in a way that two plus two equals four is not. Newman's answer only goes so far to allay this concern, but it is important

---

29. Ibid., pp. 287 and 271. Dollinger 'praises Newman's ability to trace back the organs of prejudice to first principles', quoted by Andrew Nash in the introduction to *Present Position*, LXXV, see note 40.
30. Newman, *Loss & Gain*, p. 34 (original emphasis).
31. Ibid.
32. Newman, *Development*, p. 170.
33. Ibid., p. 171.

because he uses it to explain why moral probation is still at play in a religion for which the dogmatic principle is central. He writes, 'we must distinguish between a revelation and the reception of it', and once God has revealed himself things like 'ignorance, misapprehension, unbelief ... do not at once cease'. The believer's reception of dogma thus still requires 'anxious diligence'. The difference between this and Anglican 'moral probation', however, is that the latter gives such reign to 'our freewill and responsibility' that even the apostles themselves cease to be infallible, and discretion can then be applied to almost any Christian moral stipulation at all.[34]

On the second issue of Newman offsetting system with mystery, he does not enter into sustained argument directly but makes passing remarks which show his forsaking of the compromise of the English sensibility means that system is no longer inherently problematic. Indeed, this shift in his approach to theology had been alluded to in his review of William Palmer's *Treatise on the Church of Christ* which appeared in the *British Critic* in October 1838.[35] Throughout the Second Spring period, moreover, Newman critiques a tendency he perceives in others, which he calls 'viewiness'. This refers to those who, formed on a *via media* approach to truth, take different 'views' of things at will, discerning what they view to be the good in different perspectives. The problem with this is not just superficiality, however, but error. Certain truths (most obviously, dogmatic truth) will at times not permit other perspectives in their underlying essentials or 'assumed principles'.[36] If you scrutinize someone who is 'viewy', it will soon become apparent that many of their opinions are inconsistent. This is because their opinions have not been developed into a mutually correcting coherent system. As Newman writes, to be 'viewy' is not to have undertaken the 'connection of fact with fact, truth with truth, the bearing of fact upon truth, and truth upon fact', so while they have a multitude of views, 'viewy' people 'locate nothing' because 'they have no system'. They comfort themselves with the idea this is a proof of the fact 'they are unfettered, moderate, dispassionate' and 'they observe the mean'. And, perhaps taking issue again with 'freeborn Englishmen' and perhaps even the words of Rule Britannia, he says they are in fact 'the most helpless of slaves; for our strength in this world' is to be 'captives of truth'.[37]

So viewiness is, like other corollaries of the *via media*, presented as another one of those 'grievous deficiencies' of the English. In the *Present Position* Newman arrives at a similar position yet with even more damning assertions. He says that the 'establishment of Protestantism was a comparatively easy undertaking in England' for the reason that 'there are certain peculiarities of the English character, which were singularly favourable to the royal purpose'. One of these is being naturally indisposed to 'reason' or the 'way of science'. He says Catholic theologians 'view

34. Ibid., pp. 170–1.
35. Newman, 'Palmer's Treatise'.
36. Newman, *Present Position*, p. 271.
37. Newman, *Loss and Gain*, pp. 16–18; cf. *Idea*, p. 9, for more on 'viewiness'.

Catholic truth as a whole, as one great system of which part grows out of part, and doctrine corresponds to doctrine' and they 'carry out' their doctrinal 'system' into 'its fulness'. But all this is described as 'distasteful to an Englishman', it may 'suit the Germans, and still more the French, Italians, and the Spaniards; but we ourselves ... break away from them as dry, uncertain, [and] theoretical'.[38] Ian Ker calls Newman the 'most unsystematic of theologians',[39] but this cannot include his favour of system as a principle, even if he was yet to achieve it himself.

6.3 Summary

There should be little doubt from the foregoing firstly that Newman's writings witness a significant change towards his understanding of the *via media*, which is grounded on a change in his approach to truth in relation to Catholic dogma. There is no compromise with Catholic truth, and arriving at such would mean adopting a position just as false as an outright contradiction. This is a key factor in challenging the Anglican application of the Lérinian dictum to justify the position that Antiquity speaks against Rome, for this position, applied as an example of 'Continuity of Principle', means that later developments within this commitment to dogmatic truth are as authentic as Nicaea, or Chalcedon, or even the Apostles' Creed and Holy Scripture itself.

There should equally be little doubt that Newman's forsaking of compromise is not only about ecclesiology and the epistemics of dogma but caught up in a dramatic struggle with the English sensibility itself. *Loss and Gain* and the satires make it abundantly clear that the elevation of expedience to the status of objective truth is 'a grievous sin' of England, specifically. Newman connects some of the most disturbing elements of No-Popery with this, suggesting English anti-Catholic prejudice is not merely about tribalism and patriotism. Newman argues that tendencies inherent in the English sensibility itself are to blame, particularly a fondness for free thinking, for concord and civic stability. Yet Newman realizes this self-congratulation is delusional. The self-satisfaction of the rationales for compromise mask a deeply prejudiced and embittered people who witness their own contrariness by celebrating the principle of *audi alteram partem* while being as slavish to their own assumptions as any 'sickly denizen of the hothouse'.

We can now revisit the tensions of the Tractarian Newman to summarize how the English instinct for compromise develops in Newman's life and work during and after his conversion. We can also now appreciate why it was Newman quotes the passage on the 'characteristic calmness and caution' of 'English theology' from the *Prophetical Office* in *Difficulties*, relaying that he feels 'shame and sorrow' when quoting his own words. This is because his position has so radically altered, he realized his fundamental convictions ('assumed principles') were false.[40] The

---

38. Newman, *Present Position*, p. 57.
39. Newman, *Development 2*, p. xxi.
40. Newman, *Difficulties*, p. 375.

overarching impression is thus one of a radical break or rupture from the English sensibility. In the *Prophetical Office*, Newman wants to determine the parameters of the *via media* so it does not become 'mere literature'. Now, he says that 'system' alone 'advances to philosophy and truth' as it recedes 'from poetry'.[41]

His points are expressed with a polemical ire in *Loss and Gain* and the satires, but some years later the basic point appears in more measured form in the *Idea of a University* (1852). Here, Newman frequently references equanimity as a primary virtue of the cultivated intellect. However, while he says that 'compromise' is necessary for human society and intellectual life, still there is an obvious 'limit' and 'this is found in the *proviso*' that 'there should be no sacrifice of the main object of the combination'. For otherwise the compromise is 'destructive of the principle of the combination', as must apply to the dogmatic principle of Christianity itself.[42] It is the underlying convictions which have changed with Newman's conversion. He has converted from the assumed principles of the English sensibility (*audi alteram partum*) to the assumed principles of the Catholic faith (believers are *cooperatores veritatis*). This is indeed a 'second spring' in precisely the sense that this metaphor is used in the celebrated sermon. He enters into springtime because he has to begin again from 'First Principles', like a babe in arms. This is not a developmental step arising organically from the prior trajectory of his life and work. It is an irruption of grace, of the supernatural. Therefore, when it comes to an instinct for compromise, Newman is now unabashedly un-English. Newman decides the English sensibility lay, like the paganism of old, shattered into pieces by the unassailable march of truth as dogma.

---

41. Newman, *Loss & Gain*, p. 19.
42. Newman, *Idea*, p. 23.

Chapter 7

RESERVE IN THE SECOND SPRING

Chapter 4's discussion of reserve in the Tractarian Newman showed that he is caught up in his affection for this element of Englishness rather uncritically. This is demonstrated by the fact that he brings an attribute of the English sensibility into the very centre of Christian life to the point that other aspects of that life (such as *kataphasis* and doxology) are undermined.

In this chapter, we shall see that Newman's position on various issues related to reserve move from a somewhat uncritical participation in his cultural sensibility towards a tension between that sensibility and his developing Catholic theology. That is, there are moments where he critiques his former affection for reserve, and yet that same affection appears to remain effective on other areas.

7.1 Metaphysical developments in ideas in the Development *essay*

The *Development* essay is very different in tone to *Arians*, although they share much in common being his most historically focused books, and they were written only just over ten years apart. Yet *Arians* is unmistakeably the work of a young man, and has a palpably exuberant and rhapsodic style, ironically, given the book's condemnation of linguistic effulgence. (Stephen Thomas even asks if Newman should not be considered a 'hypocrite' for so denouncing 'rhetoric, while wielding it as his own most powerful weapon'.)[1] The *Development* essay, along with his other Second Spring writings, do not focus explicitly on reserve, and this element of the English sensibility is thus much less definitive than compromise. At first glance, however, at least one particular element of an English affection for reserve seems to have endured into the conversion period, surrounding the reserve about language in relation to dogmatic formulations, language's limitations to arrive at its objects or referents when it comes to the divine.

Near the beginning of the essay, Newman outlines nine types of developments in ideas, of which the last is 'metaphysical'. He quotes at length from a sermon he preached in 1843. This passage is really just a fuller (and somewhat calmer) expression of the standpoint of reserve in relation to dogmatic formulations than

---

1. Thomas, *Newman and Heresy*, p. 253.

the more suggestive *Arians*. He says, those 'particular propositions' which 'are used to express portions' of Christianity, 'which are vouchsafed to us, can never really be confused with the idea [of Christianity] itself' because this is something 'all such propositions taken together can but reach' but 'cannot exceed'.[2] No abundance of words will exhaust divine revelation, and this is not just a difference of degree but of kind. Newman opts for quantitative rather than qualitative terms, admittedly, but these terms are being used metaphorically. When he mentions 'the dogmatic statement of the Divine Nature', for example, he affirms that words cannot capture an 'object' which is an enduring and infinite mystery. His way of describing this is to use numerical excess to capture the impossibility of the task at hand. 'Catholic dogmas' are thus described as 'symbols of a divine fact, which, far from being compassed by these propositions, would not be exhausted, not fathomed, by a thousand'. 'Creeds and dogmas,' he writes, 'are necessary only because the human mind cannot reflect on [the Divine Nature], except piecemeal.' Dogmatic statements are thus only 'expressions' of the divine, they 'are never equivalent to it'.[3]

The *Development* essay thereby maintains Newman's reserve towards dogmatic formulations, and his instinctive distrust of language. It will be recalled that, in *Arians*, the reader is confronted with such a reserved position towards the efficacy of language in dogma that it seems Newman's only grounding for the authority of dogma can be ecclesial authority, yet this is something he is then seeking to avoid as a distinctly 'Roman' position. While some commentators have suggested that Newman simply decided authority was right after all prior to converting, this is incorrect. It is rather that the *Development* essay taken as a whole answers to his concern and provides a distinctly new position. Ecclesial authority is a 'seal' or 'confirmation' upon right teaching. It is impressed upon its objects with ecclesial infallibility, undoubtedly, but not grounded on that infallible authority. It is Newman's 'seven notes of authentic development' which he considers to provide the substance for showing that the authoritative seal is indeed correct, not the seal itself. Of course this does not mean a believer can withhold assent to something sealed as authentic by ecclesial authority, it is rather that the seven notes are offered by Newman as an 'hypothesis' an inquirer can apply to be reassured that a particular development is indeed authentic.

7.2 Reserve questioned

7.2.1 The supernatural virtue of faith in Difficulties

The endurance of a reserve towards language in relation to dogma in the *Development* essay might lead some to suggest an affection for reserve simply endures in Newman's Second Spring period without modification. However, there is clear evidence of significant change in Newman's previously unquestioned

---

2. Newman, *Development*, p. 115.
3. Ibid., pp. 114–16.

celebration of reserve as a Tractarian. *Difficulties of Anglicans*, although rightly classed as a satire, features a theological interlude in which this change is technically articulated. That this is a theological interlude in an otherwise polemical text is shown by Newman's comment that he is 'obliged' against his polemical purposes 'to explain a point of doctrine'.[4] The point in question is centred on the supernatural virtue of faith. This virtue would today more often be termed a 'theological' rather than supernatural virtue, and is defined by Aquinas as 'the act of the intellect assenting to a Divine truth owing to the movement of the will, which is itself moved by the grace of God'.[5]

Faith is called 'supernatural' because it is inspired by God's grace moving the will. As put by Vatican I, 'Faith is a supernatural virtue by which we with the inspiration and assistance of God's grace, believe those things to be true which He has revealed.' Language of the 'supernatural' is of course much less common today than it was in the nineteenth century.

It is necessary to touch briefly on this to appreciate Newman's argument. Faith, hope, and love are called supernatural virtues because they are conditions or habits of grace 'implanted' into the heart by God, and not inherent to the capacities of our natural state. The word 'theological' is often used now to capture their divine initiative as expressions of God's life 'within' the terms of human life. More specifically, the same processes of cognition are at work in giving intellectual assent to the things of God as they are in giving intellectual assent to worldly matters, it is just that worldly knowledge is centred on the world, and faith arises after God graciously turns the mind to accepting revealed truth, hence faith being a 'theological' rather than a 'natural' virtue. Newman's discussion of the supernatural virtue of faith in *Difficulties* is when his training in Catholic theology becomes clearly perceptible. The nature–supernature distinction was central and unavoidable in nineteenth-century Catholic theology, and it appears in his writings from 1850 onwards.

In *Difficulties*, Newman focuses on certain corollaries of the supernatural virtue of faith which he uses to explain a profound difference between the sensibilities of England and of Catholic countries. The contrast in question is particularly instructive for this chapter, insofar as the difference centres on English reserve compared to what he termed a typically 'Mediterranean' expressiveness and vocal enthusiasm. That is, Newman seeks to convince his Anglican audience that those populations they would consider to be lacking in reserve – mentioning Spain, France, and Italy – can yet somehow be closer to God as Catholic populations, than the ever-so decorous and civilized English. Recalling Burke's comment about 'manners as things with vex and sooth, corrupt or purify, exalt or debase, barbarise or refine us', Newman acknowledges that his Oxford-educated Tractarian audience

---

4. Newman, *Difficulties*, pp. 268–9.
5. Cf. St. Thomas, II-II, Q. iv, a. 2.

must struggle with aligning traits deemed typical of, say, Spaniards and Italians with the superiority of Catholicism for which Newman is arguing. Put bluntly, if these peoples are so endowed with the grace of God, how might nineteenth-century English gentlemen make sense of their ill-mannered vulgarity? This is a difficult contention for contemporary readers to appreciate, but there are good grounds to suggest Newman is not merely setting up a rhetorical device but drawing on his own experience. He says in the *Apologia* that Froude was 'shocked by the degeneracy he thought he saw in the Catholics of Italy', for example.[6] He begins his discussion in *Difficulties* by assuming his audience is 'much offended' with 'the bad taste of Catholics abroad'. He says they find them to have 'the faults of barbarians' because 'they have no self-command'.[7] Therefore, 'no English gentleman' would want to 'make himself the co-religionist of such slaves' who are kept in the state of 'children' by their infantile religion.

He goes on, however, to argue that such assumptions are based on a woeful misunderstanding, a confusing of the natural and the supernatural. He writes that 'order, tranquillity', 'literature', and 'refinement' are but the 'world's ends' and thus distinct from the supernatural end of the Church, the salvation of souls.[8] But Newman imagines his former co-religionists objecting: 'religion is a sacred, awful, mysterious, solemn matter' and so 'it should be approached with fear, and named, as it were *sotto voce*'. One can easily imagine this sentence having been voiced by the author of *Arians* himself, but now he wants to argue that, in a certain sense, the opposite is true.[9] He goes on, 'there is a bold' and 'indelicate way' among Catholic populations 'of speaking of even points of faith' which is 'utterly out of taste and indescribably offensive to any person of ordinary refinement'. Catholics are thus described as 'rude where they should be reverent, jocose where they should be grave, and loquacious where they should be silent'. That he might include the theologically literate in this condemnation is suggested when he says that even the most 'august doctrines' are 'glibly enunciated' by them with 'some short and smart theological formulae'.[10]

Interestingly, Newman presents a concession to his audience in the admission that 'national differences' do not account for this difference. It is not enough to say that the English and the Italians have different sensibilities, for the simple reason that the same traits of irreverence, jocularity, and loquaciousness seem to be endemic in all Catholic countries. It cannot be denied, he writes, that these traits must arise from the 'character' of their religion rather than their temperaments.[11] Yet, this concession enables Newman to put such observations to work in arguing

---

6. Newman, *Apologia*, p. 105.
7. Newman, *Difficulties*, p. 230.
8. Ibid., p. 235.
9. Ibid., pp. 265–6 (insofar as Catholics 'exhibit the combine and contrary faults of profaneness and superstition').
10. Ibid., pp. 265–6.
11. Ibid., p. 268.

for the truth of the Catholic faith. He goes on to argue that it is the supernatural virtue of faith which explains the difference between Catholics and Protestants, between England and some of her near neighbours.

This virtue, in scholastic theology, is distinctly cognitive. As put by Thomas, it is 'the act of the *intellect* assenting to a Divine *truth*' (my emphasis), and is thus distinct from the more wide-reaching and existential approach to faith in much Protestant theology. Taking Luther as the most obvious example, faith is described as a 'living, bold trust in God's grace' which is all-encompassing, changing 'our hearts, our spirits, our thoughts and all our powers'. This includes of course the doing of good works, seen as flowing from and virtually indistinguishable from faith: 'It is just as impossible to separate faith and works as it is to separate heat and light from fire!'[12] Because the scholastic focus on faith as cognitive has been lost in Protestantism, says Newman, his audiences have 'no experience of this habit, this act of mind' as a discrete element in the believer's life. They therefore define it in reference to things other than the 'spiritual sight of the unseen', claiming it is 'substantially the same as obedience' or as 'the fervour and heartiness which attend good works'.[13] But, 'in a Catholic's creed', faith is a graced cognition of the things of God: 'a certainty of things not seen but revealed; caused directly by a supernatural influence on the mind from above'. This means works are to some extent separable from faith, insofar as someone can have graced cognition of the things of God even if their conduct remains thoroughly natural. Newman thus claims that 'populations baptised Catholic combine their lapsing and concupiscence with the gift of the supernatural virtue of faith'. This means they still 'have a vivid perception, like sense, of things unseen, yet have no desire at all, or affection towards them'.[14]

Faith thus endures 'in a Catholic country, on the mixed multitude, and on each of them ... is written, is stamped deep, this same wonderful *knowledge*'.[15] The endurance of this knowledge is then used to explain how it is that Catholics can speak so profanely of divine realities, so lacking in reserve and discretion. Just as the Englishman '*knows* about railroads and electric telegraphs' regardless of his 'moral state', in a Catholic country 'the ideas of heaven and hell, Christ and the evil spirit, saints, angels' and so on are straightforwardly known as self-evident facts of life: 'facts attested by each to all, and by all to each'.[16] The genteel English thus use 'vague' and palatably discrete words like 'Providence', or 'the Deity' for referring to divine things. Catholics, by contrast, 'speak of the "Sacred Heart", or of "the Mother of mercies", or of "Our Lady of Walsingham"'. But, he imagines his audiences' response to this fact: 'How unutterably profane!' he says, but this

---

12. Martin Luther, 'An Introduction to St. Paul's Letter to the Romans', in *Luther's German Bible of 1522*, translated by Robert E. Smith from *Dr. Martin Luther's Vermischte Deutsche Schriften Volume 63* (Erlangen: Heyder and Zimmer, 1854), pp. 124–5.
13. Newman, *Difficulties*, p. 269.
14. Ibid., pp. 273–4.
15. Ibid. (Original emphasis.)
16. Ibid., pp. 275–6.

is 'profane to you ... a population that only half believes', meaning they believe without the supernatural virtue of faith making divine things as concretely real as any worldly object. Moreover, one might add that strictly speaking this analysis means that what is assumed to be 'reserve', a holding back on fuller expression for reasons of decency, actually is not quite that – because the English cannot properly discern the divinity of the things under discussion, they are not holding back but are actually limited in what they discern.

7.2.2 On Marian devotion

The Newman of the Second Spring has thus indeed come a long way from *Arians*. Now reserve is not unequivocally good, but something that rather indicates a grave deficiency inherent in Protestantism, which is closer to faithlessness than faith. Indeed, as in the previous chapter, Catholicism serves as a corrective to the English sensibility on compromise, the same pattern applies to reserve: Catholicism trumps Englishness, the English must begin again from first principles, they must enter into a Second Spring. Another such moment can be seen in a comment Newman makes about one of the most well-known difficulties for nineteenth-century English converts: Marian devotion. Pusey had commented on Newman's conversion in that 'I could not imagine dear Newman writing, as the French Roman Catholic writers do, of the Blessed Virgin, and exciting the feelings by descriptions of her love and tenderness' for it 'would be an entirely different ETHOS from his sermons'.[17] Criticism of supposedly 'Italianate' or French devotions was common in Newman's day, usually connected with St Alphonsus Liguori, whose name was to crop up in the controversy preceding the *Apologia* some years later. Such writings were deemed to lack decorum, to engage in wild overstatement and sensually unseemly imagery. During the Second Spring period Newman's position on these reservations about continental devotionalism is clear. He states in a sermon from 1848 that his hearers can 'be sure of this, that if you cannot enter into the warmth of foreign books of devotion, it is a deficiency in you'.[18] As with the lack of the supernatural virtue of faith, reserve is not indicative of grace, it bespeaks a deficiency in grace.

7.2.3 A cultivated intellect in the Idea of a University

Another such moment of Catholic correction occurs in the *Idea of a University*. Here, Newman outlines a mode of educating 'gentlemen' in Liberal Education. This education is said to confer 'liberality of mind', shown by 'freedom, equitableness, calmness, moderation, and wisdom'.[19] There is strong biographical evidence that

---

17. Quoted by Cameron in Newman, *Development*, p. 20.
18. John Henry Newman, *Faith and Prejudice and Other Sermons* (New York: Sheed & Ward, 1956), p. 95.
19. Newman, *Idea*, p. 87.

Newman's Englishness was particularly perceptible during the writing of these lectures for an Irish audience. Perhaps this is one reason why he takes great care to distinguish the 'cultivated gentleman' from the person of faith. He writes, a 'Liberal Education marks out not the Christian, not the Catholic' but only 'the gentleman'. This entails that being reserved in speech does not indicate anything holy. A Liberal Education fosters 'a delicate taste, a candid, equable dispassionate mind, a noble and courteous bearing in the conduct of life' – that is, those things which Burke said must 'vex and sooth, corrupt or purify, exalt or debase, barbarise or refine us', but now Newman argues that such things are 'are no guarantee of sanctity'. In other words, being irreverent and unreserved might vex, but viewed with the eyes of faith it does not necessarily mean someone is corrupt, debased, and barbaric.

Indeed, in the *Idea* Newman goes even further, for reasons which align with his discussion of the supernatural virtue of faith in *Difficulties*. Natural virtues are described as things that can actually be dangerous, because they can be mistaken for holiness. Newman can thus state that the cultivated intellect 'concurs with Christianity in a certain way, and then diverges from it; and consequently proves in the event, sometimes its serviceable ally, sometimes, from its resemblance to it, an insidious and dangerous foe'. The issue is, of course, mistaking natural and supernatural virtues. Natural virtues have 'a special tendency ... when cultivated by beings such as we are, to impress us with a mere philosophical theory of life and conduct, in the place of Revelation'. That is, they tend to Pelagianism: 'throwing us back on ourselves, and making us our own centre, and our minds the measure of all things', for then the 'perception of the Beautiful becomes the substitute for faith'.[20]

7.3 Summary

Reserve in Newman of the Second Spring witnesses to a more complicated situation than compromise, insofar as a central aspect of reserve does endure into the *Development* essay, and is not questioned in any of the post-conversion writings – the reserve towards language in dogmatic formulations. However, as regards the supernatural virtue of faith in *Difficulties*, and backed up by his Marian sermon from 1848, an otherwise corrective pattern is at work in which Newman uses Catholicism to correct the affection for reserve of the English sensibility. In the *Idea* this goes yet further, for now he explains why reserve, along with other English virtues, can indeed be dangerous as a surreptitious form of Pelagianism.

To compare the Tractarian and Second Spring periods directly, we have seen in *Arians* that Newman extends a strategic tactic for evangelization from the Alexandrian Church into something encompassing all of Christian life. In Newman's discussion of the supernatural virtue of faith, however, the lack of

---

20. Ibid., p. 89.

reserve he says his audience observe in Catholic populations is indicative of a great spiritual gift, albeit without the cultivated affections that correspond to it. The affections are no longer to be prepared *prior to* disclosing the mysteries, and now they can continue uncultivated even in people of faith.

On the other hand, however, we have seen that in *Arians* Newman views the formulation of dogma as unfortunate but necessary, for it would be better for people to have stayed 'in that free and unsuspicious teaching' of the childhood of the Church prior to formally dogmatic statements. Here, the reserve towards language in relation to dogmatic truth endures. On the 'popular' level, or for the 'multitude', he finds 'profaneness' can be indicative of a great spiritual benefit. On the more intellectual level of formal theology, however, the tendency to reserve is celebrated as a wide-ranging and integral facet of Christian life.

There is therefore still a certain tension at play in the Newman of the Second Spring. If it is to be commended that the Catholic masses have a supernatural virtue which enables them to have a real and concrete knowledge of divine things, like the English have a real and concrete knowledge of 'railroads and electric telegrams', why does this virtue not have some bearing on the interpenetration of dogma with the thing referred to? When Newman berates his audience for preferring abstract terms like 'Providence' or 'the Deity' over against fond and tender familiarities like the 'Sacred Heart' and the 'Mother of mercies', can his reasoning not also apply to his account of dogma, to the 'God from God, light from light' of the Nicene Creed?

Focusing on reserve in the Second Spring period also throws Newman's new adoption of the nature–supernature distinction into relief. Reserve is presented as a natural good, and this is why it must be separated from the far superior supernatural good of faith. As with Marian devotion, hostility bespeaks a deficiency in grace, a deficiency in the supernatural. Indeed, the natural–supernatural distinction explains why a 'noble and courteous bearing in the conduct of life' can slip into Pelagianism, an acting as if one can be saved without grace. In this connection Newman's comment that 'the national religion' comes 'of mere nature, and its teaching is of nature' because it 'leads' to 'propriety of conduct' but 'has not the power to lead the multitude upward' to heaven is a case in point.[21] What is needed is the irruption of grace, a new heart, an entering into a new springtime in defiance of time. For the national religion 'does not engrave upon the heart, it does not inflict upon the conscience, the supernatural'.[22]

This motif of rupture or break as regards the nature–supernature distinction applies, by omission, to Newman's description of the supernatural virtue of faith in relation to the affections. In *Arians*, dogmatic teaching was 'reserved' from catechumens so their affections could be duly cultivated prior to disclosing the most sacred things of God. In *Difficulties*, it is unequivocally stated that the cultivation of the affections is not conditional for knowing divine things. Yet,

---

21. John Henry Newman, *Discourses to Mixed Congregations* (London: Longmans, Green, 1906), p. 102.
22. Ibid.

the speaking freely in faith of Catholic populations remains by Newman's own description 'profane', while graced, while supernaturally stimulated. A question which remains open is how affections might be duly cultivated on the basis of grace, with no threat of Pelagianism. As it stands, and shown by the discussion of Marian devotionalism, Newman presents impressions of profaneness as indicative of a deficiency in grace: 'It is a deficiency in you.'

When it comes to dogma, Newman remains orientated on those same natural virtues which he has begun to view with suspicion by the time he writes *Difficulties* and the *Idea*. In popular piety, the supernatural can enter into human life and transform it from within. In formal theology, it remains something grafted onto life, or rather language, and does not issue in the remaking of language itself.

Chapter 8

EMPIRICISM IN THE SECOND SPRING

Chapter 5's discussion of the empiricism of Newman's Tractarian period focused firstly on a pronounced prioritizing of action over ideas in Christian obedience seen particularly in the *Parochial and Plain Sermons*. Secondly, it gave attention to Newman's willingness to deviate from the traditional principles of common sense pragmatism in seeking to reorient Anglican ecclesiology on what is by his own admission 'an assemblage of words' hitherto under the province of 'reason': the *via media*. The Tractarian Newman broadly shares the empiricism of the English sensibility in his prioritizing of action over idea in the *Parochial and Plain Sermons*, but works against it in the *Prophetical Office*. As it stands then, his adoption of empiricism is relatively balanced, encouraged for the individual believer, but challenged when it comes to collective self-identity in Anglican ecclesiology. The task of this chapter is to discern the extent to which this adoption of English empiricism changes during the Second Spring period.

8.1 The Development *essay as an empirical inquiry*

The seismic significance of the *Development* essay for Newman's intellectual development has already been discussed in relation to the collapse of the tenability of the *via media* which Newman associates with his reading of the Fathers in 1836, 1839, and 1841. There is a further aspect of these seismic changes to be discussed here because it is highly significant for this chapter. That is, the empirical nature of the *Development* inquiry cannot be separated from the radical changes in Newman's thought. In the first place, the dominant Catholic approaches to doctrinal development were seen by Newman as unsatisfactory, because they were 'too rigid for the actual historical facts'. One example of this is what Ian Ker calls 'the "logical explication" theory' of the Scholastics, in which each development is logically implied from the doctrines which precede it, and all unfolds through deductive inference. James Cameron glosses the related approach of Bousset by saying that a believer 'assenting to transubstantiation or the double procession of the Paraclete' had already 'assented to other doctrines which logically implied these doctrines', which are presumably the hypostatic union in the first case, and the eternal begetting of the Son in the second. Newman's insistence on studying development as it occurs in empirical history and not merely foreclosing debate with a closed system of logical deduction evinces 'his determined refusal to espouse "mere theories" that ignored the untidy actualities of history and life'.[1]

The empiricism of *Development* is displayed most clearly in the opening pages of the essay, where the reader is left in little doubt as to what the locus of Newman's investigation is: the empirical reality of the Church as disclosed by history. He states, 'Christianity is no dream of the study or the cloister' because 'from the first' it has had 'an objective existence'. This is described not as a matter of historical studies alone but something pertaining to the faith itself: 'its home is in the world' and so 'to know what it is, we must seek it in the world'. The objective reality of this religion as an empirical fact enduring through time is thus said to be 'our most natural informant concerning the doctrine and worship of Christianity'.[2]

The empiricism of the inquiry is also displayed by a particular form of argumentation Newman undertakes, in which he roots his inquiry in descriptions of empirical consciousness. It would be anachronistic to call this phenomenological, but it is understandable why some have considered him to foreshadow important developments in later Continental Philosophy.[3] To describe empirical consciousness is to articulate the ways in which phenomena of consciousness (such as perceptions, ideas, or feelings) arrive and interplay in life as it is lived. It works from the perspective of the subject, from the consciousness of embodied, social life, hence empirical. Having introduced his essay, Newman writes, 'it is a characteristic of our minds to be ever engaged in passing judgements on the things that come before them'. He goes on to say that of 'the judgements thus exercised' some endure in consciousness having been subject to repeated verification by subsequent experience, becoming 'firmly fixed in our minds' so they 'have a hold over us'. Such 'habitual judgements' as regards 'views of life and the world' are classed under the heading of 'belief', and are called 'ideas'. Some of these ideas are 'representatives of things' of 'facts existing', as in the case of Christianity. He argues that when such an idea 'is held by persons who are independent of each other' and 'variously circumstanced', it can be considered 'an objective truth'. Moreover, habitual judgements develop into 'formal statements' as the judgements of multitudes of persons in different circumstances interplay and correct each other. Then 'formal statements' which have withstood the test of time 'serve to impress a fuller and more exact representation of the original upon the mind' than previously.[4] This is the sense in which one of Newman's most famous comments should be understood: 'truth is wrought by many minds working together freely'.[5] The key points here are that Newman roots his inquiry through a description of empirical consciousness in embodied, social life, and that 'the idea of Christianity'

---

1. Ian Ker in introduction to Newman, *Development 2*, pp. xx–xxi.
2. Newman, *Development*, pp. 69 and 90.
3. See Chapter 10, note 7.
4. Newman, *Development*, p. 96.
5. Newman, *Apologia*, p. 49.

accrues from empirical history: it is a reality known through an unfolding and developing constellation of habitual judgements about it.

Having discerned that Christianity is indeed an objective fact through its emergence in empirical consciousness, Newman 'tests' his approach to doctrinal development through scrutinizing empirical history to decide whether the theory can be said genuinely to pertain. His 'hypothesis' is that the authenticity of developments can be affirmed by establishing whether or not a specific development evinces the 'seven notes'. The key point for present purposes is that he tests his own hypothesis 'in' the empirical world, by establishing whether it can satisfy the demands of empirical history. This differs from, say, the aforementioned 'logical explication' approach to development, for which one's refusal to accept, say, transubstantiation, would mean there is fault with one's logical reasoning, an erroneous deduction. Significantly, history and arguably even theology then have very little bearing on what is orthodox and what is not. Indeed, as regards history, a strict logical explication approach means any development in doctrine could theoretically be discerned by a committed logician long before its historical emergence.

For Newman, however, because Christianity's 'home is in the world', developments are worldly things. They are objective events, governed by divine providence, giving rise to phenomena of consciousness, from which habitual judgements are formed, and constellations of those judgements are eventually subjected to a process of modification and correction under the auspices of the Holy Spirit. Cameron writes that Newman insisted on 'submitting his theory to the test of practice'. In logical explication, practice – that is, empirical history – is superfluous, whereas in the *Development* essay it is worldly events which are at the nexus of revelation.[6] By being verifiable by recourse to the world itself, something theoretical passes 'from being a paper religion to being a real religion'.[7]

Approaching empirical history as the primary 'informant' for understanding Christian doctrine is undoubtedly empiricist. Interestingly, however, it is precisely this element of empiricism which Newman highlights during the Second Spring period as distinctly un-English. This is shown in the *Present Position*, in the same passage discussed in Chapter 4 where Newman highlights an antipathy to 'system' as markedly English. As we have seen, he maintains that during the Reformation, 'certain peculiarities of the English character' were 'singularly favorable to the royal purpose'. Antipathy to system is joined by antipathy to 'fact', or what he calls 'the way of history'. He goes on, 'an Englishman, as is notorious, takes comparatively little interest in the manners, customs, opinions, or doings of foreign countries', and the same insularity applies to the study of 'past times and foreign countries' entailed by historical research. Hence, the Englishman is not only 'careless of abstract truth' but also 'apathetic to historical fact'.[8]

---

6. Cameron in introduction to Newman, *Development*, pp. 17–18.

7. Ibid., pp. 29–30.

8. Newman, *Present Position*, pp. 57–63.

This is indeed a surprising observation. Empiricism is an overarching orientation to worldly reality, and the study of history involves discerning the truth of bygone worldly realities in order to understand them and the present. But Newman does not mean that the English tradition favours some less empirical approach to the past, say a mythological or idealistic, schematic approach. The issue is that English empiricism is for him a concern with the empirical *present*, the living here-and-now. He arrives at this position by pointing out that, for all the Englishman's antipathy to foreign lands, he is equally known for his welcoming generosity to foreign sojourners in his own country. This is, he claims, indicative of the fact 'we [the English] look at what is immediately before us' and so 'care little for the past; we resign ourselves to current circumstances'. As evidence, he points out that 'English divines' have cared 'as little for ecclesiastical history' as they have for 'theological science'.[9] This highly individual line of reasoning seems to suggest Newman is in the midst of conflicting impulses. Pragmatism as a sensitivity to continuous development through time is something seen as central to Englishness during his Tractarian days. Newman at the time of Second Spring now considers the empirical tradition of England to be a concern with the present at the expense of the past. This antipathy to historical fact gives further ammunition to his case that English Reformation was no moderate or cautious 'middle path', it was no careful adjustment on the basis of the accumulation of circumstances which preceded it. It was rather a radical break with all that went before it, and it was successful because the Englishman happily dismisses history: This 'temper of Englishmen', this antipathy to the past, thus 'fits with the exigencies of Protestantism'.[10]

Newman's comments on a concern with empirical history being un-English mean his own *Development* essay is an outlier from the English tradition, which would perhaps explain some of why the writing of this essay led him to decide to become a foreigner in his own land by converting. Newman's adoption of 'foreignness' is further indicated by the fact he even argues that deductive logic – that other un-English method – is the exclusive method of theology itself in the *Idea of a University*. Notwithstanding his deeply empirical alternative to scholastic explication in relation to studying the development of doctrine, some five years after the publication of the *Development* essay he writes that theology has one 'intelligible method' which issues 'in necessary and immutable results'. That is, 'deduction *only* is the instrument of Theology', and 'the inferential method' is 'its sole instrument'.[11] The *Development* essay itself, as historical, if it relies on any particular method of induction, would be the more empirically attuned abductive inference to best explanation, hence Newman calls his 'seven notes' an hypothesis. It is thus apparent that now Newman's acceptance of his training in Rome even takes pre-eminent place over the theological reasoning that led him there.

---

9. Ibid., p. 58.
10. Ibid.
11. Newman, *Idea*, pp. 55 and 154 (my italics).

8.2 Industry in Difficulties *and the* Present Position

We have seen that nineteenth-century English industrial ascendency is commonly linked with the empirical disposition of the English sensibility, both in the broader tradition, and by Newman himself, who calls the English 'an active race'. This proves important in *Difficulties*, where Newman acknowledges this observation, but seeks to show his Anglican audience that the purportedly impractical and backward nature of the populations of Catholic countries can by no means be used as any reflection of the benefits of the Catholic Church. This accompanies his argument from the supernatural virtue of faith, but here the focus is Britain as the cradle of industrialization. As Andrew Nash writes, English anti-Catholicism was linked with the self-confidence of the nation 'which had invented the Industrial Revolution' and 'saw itself as the vanguard of social progress'.[12] As put by James Cameron, 'it was the common sense of Englishmen' that England 'owed' 'an assurance of almost unlimited material progress to her Protestantism'.[13] This pervasive sentiment was based on a variety of intersecting assumptions about Catholicism. Catholicism was seen as childish and superstitious, so inimical to liberality of thought and inquiry; it was seen as otherworldly and ethereal, and so not concerned with practical improvements to society, it was seen as being governed by a corrupt and sinister priestly caste, and therefore hostile to progress and reform.

Newman pours scorn on such prejudice, pointing to the asininity of considering social states of affairs to be the measure of a religion. He says the Catholic Church is concerned only with the salvation of souls, it distinguishes this heavenly end from all 'the world's ends'.[14] In one of the most earnest passages of his satirical writings, he states, 'she would rather save the soul of one single wild bandit of Calabria, or whining beggar of Palermo, than draw a hundred lines of railroad through the length and breadth of Italy, or carry out a sanitary reform' in 'every city of Sicily'.[15] The English are accused of making a category error when they judge the fruits of the Church to be industrial and social progress. Not 'till the State is blamed for not making saints', he writes, may it be 'the fault of the Church that she cannot invent a steam engine'. He goes on to mock the presumption of English self-understanding. Perhaps the English are a people 'full of ability and energy' in 'professions or trade', 'skilled in the mechanical arts', and a 'hard-working, money making community', he writes. Yet 'the Church knows well' that spiritually this people are no different from the Calabrian bandits. They are still mired in 'a state of continual lapse from the centre of sanctity and love', forever 'tending to a state of habitual alienation' from God.[16] Thus, the virtues of 'faith, purity, and charity'

---

12. Sheridan Gilley in introduction to Newman, *Present Position*, p. vii.
13. Cameron, in introduction to Newman, *Development*, pp. 10–11.
14. Newman, *Difficulties*, p. 235.
15. Ibid., p. 240.
16. Ibid., pp. 240–4.

must never be mistaken for those 'virtues of a political or mercantile character' so beloved of mid-Victorian England.[17]

As with the aforementioned antipathies to system and to history, this provides further reasoning for what he terms in the *Present Position* 'the temper of Englishmen' being so suited to established Protestantism. Because they are an 'active race' so given to industry, they have by nature 'an innate veneration for merit, talents, rank, wealth, [and] science'. Because they are 'merchants, traders, and men of business', they consider political and mercantile virtues superior to humility and charity. This is why they could not resist replacing devotion to the most high God with 'loyalty to the Sovereign'.[18] Again, therefore, the 'peculiarities of the English character' explain the establishment of Protestantism during the English Reformation. Here again, an aspect of empiricism is at fault. A blindness to the past occasioned by a fixation on the empirical present combines and intensifies with their self-confidence in the merits of industrious and active endowments.

8.3 Pragmatism and law in Difficulties

Difficulties of Anglicans makes numerous satirical sideswipes at the British legal establishment. As we have seen, 'common law' has long been associated with the common sense pragmatism of English empiricism. Newman's questioning of this pragmatism towards Anglican ecclesiology is now extended to the political and juridical establishment of England itself. The event behind Newman's complaints was the Gorham controversy of 1847, when the Anglican Bishop of Exeter, Henry Philpotts, refused to institute George Gorham as vicar because he did not believe in baptismal regeneration. Gorham's view was what Newman would consider 'extreme Protestant', that faith alone lent validity to infant baptism, and it is by faith alone that a believer joins with Christ's body; the sacrament was conditional on faith. From early in his theological development, Newman had maintained the Catholic view that baptism itself confers regeneration and membership of the Church. After much wrangling, the matter was eventually escalated to the supreme legal authority of the land, the Privy Council, who ruled in Gorham's favour, citing the twenty-fifth of the thirty-nine Articles, focusing on the words referring to those who 'worthily receive' the sacraments being those in whom 'they have a wholesome effect or operation'.

Recalling that *Difficulties* began life as a series of lectures to his Tractarian fellow travellers, Newman makes frequent reference to the Privy Council's decision as uncontestable evidence that any hopes for a supposed 'Catholic cause' within the Church of England are utterly dashed. Moreover, as far as Newman is concerned, the Gorham decision points not only to the unequivocal failure of 'the movement of 1833' but also gets to the nub of why the movement was doomed from the

---

17. Ibid., p. 246.
18. Newman, *Present Position*, pp. 61 and 168.

start. In the first place, he presents the Gorham judgement as unequivocal proof that the Tractarian view of the Church of England has no purchase in the realm of empirical reality: 'Whatever ... be the abstract claims of the Anglican cause,' he writes, 'the living community to which they belong has for centuries ignored and annulled them.'[19] This shows why it was 'the judges of the Queen's Bench' that 'refused to prohibit execution of the Royal decision in the appeal made for the Bishop of Exeter'.[20] Secondly, this also showed that the English tradition itself could not be modified and sanctified by pragmatic adjustment, by cautiously altering the direction of the 'accumulation of practice and precedent', because the fault lies at the very root. Here is one of those recourses to a scheme of organic development which is so central to Newman's way of thinking: 'As physical life assimilates to itself, or casts off, whatever it encounters, allowing no interference with the supremacy of its own proper principles, so it is with life social and civil.' The Catholic doctrine of baptismal regeneration was thus shown to be alien to the intrinsic nature of the English constitutional establishment. As common law is linked to common sense, he says the chief justice spoke 'the language of reason and common sense' in relaying his judgement. The Tracts had thus fallen on deaf ears, indeed, upon those without ears *to* hear.

There is a third factor at play in this. The reason the message of baptismal regeneration cannot assimilate to the tradition is because the things of nationhood – attributes of an English sensibility – have been mistaken for the things of God. The freeborn Englishman ratifies even the decision of God's election: 'May not the free-born, self-dependent, animal mind of the Englishman choose his religion for himself?'[21] In this sense, 'the Anglican formularies' are 'but the expression of national sentiment'.[22] As Carlton says in *Loss and Gain*, they 'speak the language of common sense'.[23] Above all, there is in the decision of the Privy Council that tension between truth and expedience so central to Newman's recanting of the *via media*. The decision was made, we read, with the prime minister's commendation about deciding what would give 'general satisfaction'.[24] If baptismal regeneration as defined by the Tractarians had been adhered to, this would have constituted 'a suicidal act' alienating that half of the country that is unbaptized from its own religion.[25] The Anglican Church is just 'what the nation is', and thus even the doctrine of God is in the hands of mere 'lawyers'.[26]

This fury towards the establishment provides material for explaining why it is that Newman so mercilessly calls for a repenting of the common law tradition of

---

19. Newman, *Difficulties*, p. 18.
20. Ibid., p. 188.
21. Ibid., p. 24.
22. Ibid., p. 19.
23. Newman, *Loss & Gain*, p. 223.
24. Newman, *Difficulties*, p. 24.
25. Ibid.
26. Ibid., pp. 24 and 26.

pragmatic adjustment to existing circumstances having any bearing on ecclesial matters. We come back again to the defining characteristic of the Second Spring period: the English sensibility has usurped the place of God; national identity has been mistaken for divine filiation; an essentially constitutional, legal body is masquerading in the guise of God's own church. The English Reformation renders all that follows it entirely worthless, what 'profit, though ninety-nine links in the chain be sound, if the topmost is broken'?.[27]

8.4 Summary

The passages of Newman's Second Spring writings discussed here include some of his most wholehearted rebukes of those characteristics he considers distinctively English, centred on English empiricism. When it comes to popular understandings of national attributes in relation to the Industrial Revolution and the legal, parliamentarian tradition, Newman most ferociously argues his case that Englishness is at fault, that the presumptive nature of the English had led them to usurp the place of God with the place of culture. The sole exception to this is the overarchingly empirical focus of the *Development* essay, especially when contrasted with the then-dominant explicatory logic of development in Roman scholasticism. But even the study of history is presented by Newman in the *Present Position* as an empiricism which is un-English, as if he wants to claim the very essay which led to his conversion is an outlier from the common tradition of England itself.

We thus have another example of how the Second Spring evinces repeated references to a clear break with the past. This alludes not only to Newman's own break, his conversion, but gets to the nub of roundly dismissing the merit of any approach centred on pragmatic adjustment to a continuous tradition. Indeed, the Second Spring itself is a metaphor, an image, for what Newman believes is happening with the restoration of the hierarchy and the increasing numbers of his countrymen and women following him to the Tiber. The 'spring' is a break, something without precedent. It refers to something entirely alien to the tradition of the country taking hold of it, supervening over any existing circumstances – it is the death knell of any faith in pragmatic adjustments leading people to God. This is why it is described as almost unnatural, or rather supernatural. While the material world ebbs and flows, and exhibits 'order', 'constancy', and 'perpetual renovation', what he terms the 'moral world', meaning politics, society, and religion, tends only to 'dissolution' and decay. What has happened, he claims, is divine intervention in the usually unassailable process of dissolution in human affairs: 'something strange is passing over this land', he writes, 'without parallel' and 'more violent than has happened here for centuries'. It is 'a prodigious' and 'preternatural event', an 'innovation' and 'a miracle'. For 'the English Church was, and then the English Church was not, and the English Church is once again'.

---

27. Newman, *Present Position*, p. 88.

The Second Spring itself is an event outside the pattern of organic development which governs English life, because 'grace can, where nature cannot' – and that faith in the accumulation of practice and precedent was but a mere belief in nature, in the natural aptitudes of Englishness, and not faith in the grace of God. In this, the prioritizing of action over idea of the earlier *Parochial and Plain Sermons* seems difficult to sustain. Recall that, for Newman, action tends to faith because each shares an analogous epistemic character, they both require an acceptance of 'the indefinite range of God's operations beyond our means of apprehending them'. Now, action seems unlikely to lead to faith because it negates resolution and knowledge. Indeed, there is a subtle threat of Pelagianism that could arise from this, insofar as some might make faith conditional on self-sacrificial action, although Newman takes care not to commit this error himself. We come back again to an irruption of grace which supervenes over pre-existing conditions, and this applies to the pre-existent conditions of a national sensibility – grace supervenes over Englishness itself.

Chapter 9

COMPROMISE IN THE MATURE NEWMAN

The trajectory of compromise in Newman's work begins with discussions of the *via media* in the *Tracts* and the *Prophetical Office*. There, we saw firstly Newman's argument that the English 'indeterminateness' of the *via media* safeguards the freedom and discernment of Christian 'moral probation' against legalistic adherence. Secondly, that same 'indeterminateness' he calls 'characteristic' of English theology is praised for preserving a sense of God as 'mystery'; not pre-emptively 'inserting' God into a 'system'. However, we also saw Newman run into difficulties by utilizing indeterminateness against legalism and system, while the modus operandi of the *Prophetical Office* is, conversely, to determine the terrain under discussion: he seeks to render the *via media* determinate as 'positive doctrine'.

In the Second Spring period, the trajectory changes course. Newman directly takes issue with his own 'moral probation' argument in the *Development* essay, and praises 'system', not only as a great strength of Catholicism but as something indicative of its 'dogmatic principle'. Moreover, he staunchly criticizes the *via media* as unduly rooted in characteristics of the 'English mind', indicative of the obstinacy associated with the tradition of 'free born Englishmen', and fostering the hypocrisy of proclaiming *audi alteram partem* while also exhibiting deeply anti-Catholic prejudice. He similarly highlights antipathy to system as distinctly English in a negative way, grounded in the widely acknowledged English hostility to abstract reason, or what he calls 'the way of science'. Typically for his writings from this period, then, the English sensibility seems, like 'the paganism of old', to have been 'shattered into pieces by the unassailable march of the truth'.

Mapping the trajectory of English compromise in Newman's mature writings presents three foci. Firstly, Newman's account of the 'event of 1841' as described in the *Apologia*. Secondly, a revisiting of the relationship between system and mystery, not least because Newman is frequently assumed to be an 'unsystematic' theologian who was pivotal for the rediscovery of 'mystery' in twentieth-century theology.[1] Thirdly, the controversy surrounding papal infallibility and the Vatican

---

1. See Dennis Robinson, 'Preaching', in *The Cambridge Companion to John Henry Newman*, edited by Ian Ker and Terrence Merrigan, pp. 241–54, 247. For an example of the properly nuanced understanding of mystery and indeed the full influence of Newman on

Council of 1869–70 requires scrutiny, because Newman revisits the tradition of 'free born Englishmen' which is closely related to compromise through the idea that *audi alteram partem* preserves the autonomy of individual subjects against dictatorial extremes. Moreover, Newman is often assumed to have imported the principles of the *via media* with his cautious and reserved position to defining papal infallibility, which might suggest Newman reaches a rapprochement with this element of the English sensibility.

9.1 Truth as a virtue and the Apologia

9.1.1 The Kingsley controversy and Englishness

That which is distinctive in Newman's mature account of 'the event of 1841' is rooted in the circumstances which occasioned the *Apologia*: a passing remark by Charles Kingsley in a review of Froude's famously anti-Catholic *History of England* from Macmillan's magazine in January 1864. Kingsley writes,

> Truth, for its own sake, had never been a virtue with the Roman clergy. Father Newman informs us that it need not, and on the whole ought not to be; that cunning is the weapon which Heaven has given to the saints wherewith to withstand the brute male force of the wicked world which marries and is given in marriage.[2]

Newman wrote to the publishers complaining of 'grave and gratuitous slander', and, having been forwarded the letter, Kingsley replied to Newman directly. During further correspondence Newman grew increasingly incensed that Kingsley did not appear to heed the gravity of his slander, and after his final fiery letter, Kingsley responded with a pamphlet entitled 'What, then, Does Dr Newman Mean?' This pamphlet is a full-scale account of Newman's dishonesty in defence of Kingsley's original remark quoted above. Between April and July of that year, Newman wrote and published a series of pamphlets defending himself against Kingsley's allegations, which were collated and published as the *Apologia pro vita sua*.

Various notions of Englishness are at work in the Newman–Kingsley correspondence. Kingsley's original remark of course plays on the stereotype of Catholics as dishonest and to be treated with suspicion, related to assumptions about a corrupt and sinister priestly caste mentioned in the previous chapter. There is also that sense that a free-thinking, free-born Englishman could never suffer the servility of the Catholic mind in its loyalty to the pope, and that this servility is itself unmanly and infantile. Good English society thus has a 'brute male force' one never sees in a celibate priest, with marriage assumed to be the crown of mature

---

Vatican II, see Andrew Meszaros, *The Prophetic Church: History and Doctrinal Development in John Henry Newman and Yves Congar* (Oxford: Oxford University Press, 2016).

2. Newman, *Apologia*, p. 4.

manhood and independence. Kingsley's review of Froude's book includes the claim that medieval Europe suffered 'deep demoralization' because 'the Pope of Rome' had arrogated to himself the authority to define 'truth and falsehood' by 'setting his seal to a bit of parchment', thus having authority even over objective truth.[3] He claims that, a generation after the Reformation, having 'grown-up and died with the Bible in their hands', 'Englishmen and Germans began to understand (what Frenchmen and Italians did not understand)', namely, 'that they were to be judged by the everlasting laws of a God who was no respecter of persons'. Kingsley hereby attacks Tractarianism too; English Christianity begins after the Reformation, not with St Augustine of Canterbury. The 'heap of lies' which is Catholicism, writes Kingsley, had been 'accumulating' from 'ever since the first monk ... dug the first heathen Anglo-Saxon out of his barrow'.[4]

Newman's second letter mocks Kingsley as 'an educated man, breathing English air', that is, as someone from whom more equanimity and liberality of thought is expected. Lest we forget that Burke's manners which 'barbarise or refine us' do so by what Burke describes as an 'insensible operation, like that of the air we breathe'. As he has done before, Newman uses compromise as a way to ask whom the true Englishman really is: the one voicing an extreme accusation ungrounded in fact, or the accused.[5] Kingsley's penultimate letter acknowledges this slight to his gentlemanly conduct and rebukes it, saying, 'I have done as much as one English gentleman can expect from another', meaning his conduct fulfils the implied expectations but Newman's conduct is unbecoming of an English gentleman.

Kingsley's pamphlet also asks if Newman had not insinuated that 'Queen Victoria's government was to the Church of England what Nero's or Diocletian's was to the Church of Rome'. He states that it was 'notorious to all England' that the young men who heard the Oxford sermon upon which he grounds his accusations would be 'injured in their straightforwardness and truthfulness', thus bringing 'misery and shame into many an English home'. The pamphlet tempers Kingsley's first sweeping rebuke of all 'Roman clergy' in the original remarks, but still maintains there should be 'a strong distrust of certain Catholics' who become 'proselytising priests' like Newman, for they have 'turned round upon their mother Church (I had almost said their mother country) with contumely and slander'. Kingsley's parenthesized qualification is a serious matter for Victorian society. He skirts as close as he can to an accusation of treason.

Turning to the rhetorical style of *Difficulties*, Kingsley says Newman engages in 'subtle paradoxes' and 'rhetorical exaggerations' which 'whenever he touches on the question of truth and honesty' shows his taking 'a perverse pleasure in saying something shocking to plain English notions'. One of Kingsley's evidences of Roman dishonesty is St Alphonsus di Liguori, who was particularly egregious

---

3. Ibid., p. 3.
4. Ibid., pp. 3–4.
5. This is precisely the reasoning behind the comments about *audi alteram partem* in *Loss & Gain*, and the *British Critic* article 'Elliot's Travels'.

in English eyes on account not only of that aforementioned 'Mariolatry' but also an allegedly dubious approach to truthfulness in his confessional manuals. He was thus considered a paradigmatic example of the 'Roman Casuists'. All this reaches something of a crescendo when Kingsley prefaces a discussion of comments by Newman on religious sisters whose earnestness had led to self-inflicted stigmata by saying, his words 'will arouse in every English husband, father, and brother' the 'same feelings it aroused in me'. These are words he says will haunt him 'as long as Englishmen know how to guard the women whom God loves'.[6]

Newman writes the *Apologia* to defend his integrity, of course, but he states that in order to do this he must address certain presuppositions about him which are endemic among the English. It is not just that Kingsley 'called me a *liar*', he says, it was that this accusation seemed 'to the English public a plausible arraignment'. His being in an 'un-English communion' is not the main problem: the 'strength of the case' against him lies not in Kingsley's 'articles of impeachment' but in the 'bias of the court' of public opinion. The issue at stake is the sensibility of the English mind which renders it instinctively hostile to Catholicism. He calls this 'the state of the atmosphere', again reminiscent of Burke's 'air we breathe': an amorphous and subtle combination of dispositions and habits of mind. He says it is this 'atmosphere', this sensibility, that creates the 'prepossession against me' he must correct.[7]

Kingsley's attempt to destroy Newman's reputation roundly failed, and the reception of Newman's *Apologia* is unanimous in considering it victorious. As William Oddie writes, 'everyone agreed' that Kingsley's 'defeat had been crushing'.[8] Owen Chadwick states that the book 'altered the subconscious portrait of a Roman Catholic priest in the minds of many educated Britons', as 'sinister, sly, and underhand'. The same applies to the portrait of a Catholic laity as 'superstitious and credulous'.[9] Indeed, the *Apologia* has become a classic of English letters, and is read by many without giving much attention to Kingsley's remarks. This is partly because Newman rearranged the order of the text for its second reprint. Originally, the correspondence and Kingsley's pamphlet preceded Newman's responses, and Newman's later 'cuts in the text', according to William Oddie, 'have had a distorting, even a sentimentalizing effect'.[10] This reordering has arguably also led to a downplaying of the allegations of un-Englishness at play in the correspondence. It is also a widely held view that, in the *Apologia*, Newman reaches the summit of beauty with his 'silver veined' prose.[11] No commentators deny James Cameron's comment that the book ensured his 'position is secure' and

---

6. Charles Kingsley in Newman, *Apologia*, pp. 14, 28, 30, 31–2, 40–1, 45.
7. Newman, *Apologia*, pp. 81–2.
8. William Oddie in introduction to *Apologia*, p. xx.
9. Owen Chadwick, *Newman* (Oxford: Oxford University Press, 1983), pp. 64–5.
10. Oddie in introduction to *Apologia*, p. xxiii.
11. A famous phrase associated with Newman's prose based on James Joyce's statement that 'Nobody has written English that can be compared with Newman's cloistered silver veined prose'.

he was rightly 'vindicated'.[12] Newman's victory, combined with the re-ordering of the text and its aesthetic appeal, means little attention has been given to the substance of Kingsley's original accusations. The *Apologia* is thus often read as straightforward autobiography. Yet, while there is little scope to rehabilitate Kingsley, there is scope to ask how Kingsley got things so wrong.[13] That is, a subsidiary factor in those accusations is that Kingsley misappropriated Newman's position on truth in relation to the *via media*, and thereby misread his utilization of English compromise.

9.1.2 Truth as a virtue and the Apologia

Kingsley accuses Newman and 'Roman clergy' more generally of holding that 'truth, for its own sake, had never been a virtue'. Now, notwithstanding the inaccuracy of the complaint, let us call to mind that in his *Prophetical Office* Newman describes the *via media* by saying that 'virtue lies in a mean, in a point, almost invisible to the world, hard to find, acknowledged but by the few'.[14] This classically Aristotelian reference to virtue of course recalls the virtue of 'truthfulness', insofar as 'truth' itself cannot be a 'mean', but the human approximation *to* the truth can be, which is indicated by Newman's 1877 introduction to the third text saying, 'veracity, like other virtues lies in a mean', with reference to when occasions of politeness or professional necessity require that the full truth of a matter is not disclosed for fear of causing harm.[15] Truth itself, however, the accurate portrayal of objective reality, can never be a mean, any more than saying $2 + 2 = 20$ is 'truer' than $2 + 2 = 40$.

Truth itself is not a mean, and his great realization of 1841 is that truth can lie 'with the extreme party' and not in compromising between opposing positions. When describing his conversion in the *Apologia*, then, Newman needs to ensure that he cannot be misunderstood as claiming 'truth is not a virtue', while claiming that truth does not lie in a mean. The description of 'the event of 1841' in the *Apologia* thus leaves no possibility for the reader to mistake that the *via media* being 'absolutely pulverized' could mean that truth is not a virtue. To understand how he does this, it is necessary first to bear in mind a distinction in the semantics of the English word virtue. Virtue has two applications. It can mean virtue in the sense of the original ἀρετή of Aristotle, a habituated response on the mean between extremes, as in 'veracity' or truthfulness lying between the extremes of overstatement and understatement. However, virtue can also mean a more generic 'advantage' or 'benefit', something that is simply good, as in the virtue of 'eating well' or of 'religion'. It is in this second sense that Newman interprets Kingsley's 'truth, for its own sake, as a virtue', meaning the truth is always the good, there

---

12. J. M. Cameron, *John Henry Newman* (London: Longmans, Green, 1956), pp. 33–4.

13. This is by no means to agree with Frank Turner's reading of the *Apologia* as a book which questions Newman's integrity, cf. Turner, *Newman*.

14. Newman, *Prophetical Office*, p. 41.

15. Ibid., p. 59.

is virtue in truth and vice in dishonesty. This distinction is behind Newman's comment in his letter to Kingsley that 'Truth is the same in itself and in substance for Catholic and Protestant', that is, truth as objective reality, a virtue in the generalized sense of being a 'good'. But Newman distinguishes this from a virtue as ἀρετή by saying, 'There is a broad difference between a virtue, considered in itself as a principle of rule [such as "truth is always is good for its own sake"], and the application or limits of it in human conduct', such as occasions of politeness or professional necessity mentioned above. Then truthfulness does lie between extremes according to circumstance.[16]

A second distinction is at play, between the underlying presupposition of the *via media* on the one hand, and the content of it on the other.[17] That is, Newman argues that truth for its own sake underlies his experiments with the *via media* just as much as it does his conversion to Rome, there is 'continuity of principle'. The idea that he was some sort of closet Roman while preaching at Oxford ('doing the work of hostile Church in the bosom of the English establishment') is untenable, he claims, because he did not go from valuing truth (the accurate portrayal of objective reality) to considering Rome better than, or above, the truth. He went from considering the content – that which *is* true – to be found in different places, while equally assuming truth to be a good all along the way.[18] That truth is a virtue (advantage or benefit) for its own sake is thus consistent throughout his work, he claims, that which changes is what he held actually to *be* true, not any commitment to truth as such.

This distinction underlies Newman's argument that 'the principle of dogma' was at the centre of his conversion to evangelical Christianity as a teenager, his 'battle with Liberalism' as a Tractarian, and was to remain central for his life as a Catholic: 'I have changed my mind in many things', he writes, 'in this I have not … what I held in 1816, I held in 1833, and I hold in 1864'.[19] This principle is best expounded in *Development*, thus: truth is 'one, unalterable, consistent, imperative, and saving'.[20] The *Prophetical Office* seeks to find that one dogmatic truth as held by Antiquity, through the balancing of what is deemed true in either Romanism or Popular Protestantism. As he states, hitherto the *via media* was vague and undefined, a mere 'receding from extremes', but he had 'drawn it out into a definite shape and a character' precisely to show how it was 'one, intelligent and consistent'.[21] The *via media* was thus for him 'the representative of dogma' at that stage in his life.[22] This undertaking, he goes on, 'implied no doubt' of the

16. Newman, *Apologia*, pp. 8–9.
17. Cf. 'on my conversion, I was not conscious of any change in me of thought or feeling as regards matters of doctrine; this, however, was not the case as regards some matters of fact'. Ibid., p. 324.
18. Ibid., p. 80.
19. Ibid., p. 122.
20. Newman, *Development*, p. 352.
21. Newman, *Apologia*, p. 137.
22. Ibid., p. 245.

principle of dogma, meaning the commitment to truth for its own sake.[23] Truth remains throughout a 'good', a virtue in the sense of Kingsley's original remark.

These distinctions are vital for understanding Newman's argument against that accusation he says most infuriated him: 'untruthfulness'.[24] The emphases of the description of 'the event of 1841' in the *Apologia* should be understood against the background of the distinctions just described. In *Difficulties*, as we have seen, Newman describes his startling realization that the 'middle party' was just as heretical as the heretics proper of both the Monophysite and Arian controversies. In the *Apologia*, however, Newman focuses more on his reading of Wiseman's article on the Donatist controversy, and St Augustine's '*Securus judicat orbis terrarum*'. The Donatists were a local church, at variance from the universal church. St Augustine takes issue with them precisely for this local variance. Newman thus decides that universality necessitates 'the theory of the *via media* was absolutely pulverized', because it was a local variation on that truth which he has seen as 'one' and 'unalterable' by definition since 1816, so Donatism – and any English local variation to the *orbis terrarum* – must therefore be untrue.[25]

The effect of not making the moment the *via media* was 'absolutely pulverized' the same juncture as *Difficulties* – when he realized 'the truth lay … with the extreme party' – safeguards Newman against misreadings that could arise from both the distinctions at play in how the word 'truth' could be understood in relation to his earlier account of his conversion. In the first place, it defends him against the accusation that truth is not a virtue, as in ἀρετή, although this is actually almost the case.[26] The account in *Difficulties* could inadvertently lead in this direction, for in the *Prophetical Office* Newman introduces the *via media* by saying 'virtue lies in a mean', and then later realizes truth does not lie in the mean but with 'the extreme party', so truth is in this precise sense not a virtue, objective reality is not ἀρετή. However, this was perilously close to sounding like Kingsley's accusation that truth 'had never been a virtue with the Roman clergy', and thus needed careful reworking.

Secondly, there is a potential misreading arising from neglecting the distinction between truth as an underlying presupposition of the *via media*, and the content: the question of what is true as opposed to Pilate's 'what is truth?' Not only does Newman avoid any misapprehension about him changing his ideas about truth itself by focusing on the *securus*-maxim rather than discussions about truth as a mean, this same maxim entails by definition that truth is to be found in the universal Church and not in any local ecclesial community at variance with that Church. The consistency of a 'continuity of principle' is thus assured, there can be no doubt about truth being 'one' and 'unalterable' – and moreover, it is precisely the oneness and inalterability of truth which means, by definition, truth must

---

23. Ibid., p. 138.
24. Ibid., p. 73.
25. Ibid., p. 174.
26. Ibid., p. 193.

reside with the universal Church and not in a district of North Africa nor indeed Canterbury. The quest for truth is thus presented as that which drives Newman's conversion to Rome, where it concludes: truth 'for its own sake'.

Newman hammers the point home later in the book, when he describes his painful anguish about the effect his conversion would have on the young minds of Oxford. He feared his recanting of the *via media* would place in jeopardy the anti-dogmatic principle that truth is one and unalterable, and so be a victory for Liberalism. The *via media* had been seen by him as 'the representative of dogma', as a way to present Anglicanism as a 'dogmatic faith'. What pained him more than anything, we read, was the danger that 'dogmatic faith' *itself* would be swept away as he was 'breaking the *via media* to pieces'. Much hard work would be lost, because 'it is not at all easy to wind up an Englishman to a dogmatic level', and yet he had managed to do so 'in good measure'. There was now a grave danger that his conversion could 'unsettle' people's 'confidence in truth and falsehood as external things'.[27] As it stands, however, hindsight allows him to conclude this fear was unfounded. I would contend, however, that it inadvertently laid him open to wrongful accusations like Kingsley's, to the view that Newman himself doubted that truth was a real, attainable thing rather than something dictated by the mere whims of the 'Pope of Rome' setting his seal on 'a bit of parchment'.

A fair reading of the *Prophetical Office* and the *Apologia* combined suggest Kingsley got things wrong partly because of the semantic fluidity of the English language, which, combined with an innate hostility to Catholicism among the English intelligentsia, led to a woefully inaccurate portrayal of Newman's integrity. There is a particular sense in which Newman does recant the view that truth is a virtue of the *Prophetical Office*, perhaps explaining why he adopts the common Roman term 'veracity' for this virtue in his edited reprint of the same book in 1877. In the *Apologia*, Newman needed to emphasize the continuity and organically developing trajectory of his thought, which Turner describes as his Catholic faith 'emerging from a Protestant chrysalis'.[28]

9.1.3 Anglicanism as a 'halfway house'

In terms of Englishness and English compromise, the impression of the Second Spring writings is that any remnant of 'compromise' as a good in itself was untenable, and that this instinct for compromise is actually rooted in English presumption and self-confidence. There is nothing in the writings of the mature Newman to suggest that holding fast to truthfulness or veracity as a mean can in any way be taken as an attempt to recover English compromise. Newman states that 'truthfulness' stands under 'the jurisdiction of mankind at large', any member of which has 'the right to judge' in the case 'of a Catholic, of a Protestant, of an Italian, or of a Chinese'.[29] Yet in the *Apologia* Newman does introduce a new element to

27. Ibid., pp. 244–6.
28. Turner, *John Henry Newman*, p. 6.
29. Newman, *Apologia*, p. 73.

his thinking which is a second focus of this chapter, and which makes for a more conciliatory tone towards Anglicanism and Englishness. Newman describes the *via media* as a 'halfway house' on the way to Catholicism, for it has the dogmatic principle, and considers that principle to be partially displayed by the Church of Rome. Strictly speaking, Newman will always maintain after 1841 that truth as an objective reality has no 'halfway house', for to say 2 + 2 = 20 is no nearer the truth than saying 2 + 2 = 40. But in the existential trajectory of a human life we do experience varying proximities to truth, and can thus speak of differences of degree.

Indeed, Newman says against Kingsley that 'if truth be a real objective thing' then changes of mind are intrinsically '*necessary*', because no-one is born in possession of the fulness of truth. This should 'comfort a person who has been brought-up in a system *short* of truth', he says, meaning a system partially true rather than entirely errant. He asks, 'may we not ... seek a blessing *through* obedience even to an erroneous system, and guidance by means of it out of it?'.[30] In a long discussion of the Anglican Church towards the end of the book, Newman continues to strike a much more conciliatory tone than the Second Spring writings, and these occasioned criticisms from his fellow converts. He admits firstly to 'recognise in the Anglican Church' an institution which is 'to a certain point, a witness and teacher of religious truth'. Secondly, he writes that it has been 'a serviceable breakwater against doctrinal errors, more fundamental than its own'.[31]

The above quotations are important because there is a shift between the Second Spring and the mature writings here. In the *Present Position* Anglicanism is condemned as rooted in 'assumed principles' of Englishness, it is errant at the outset, and its developing trajectory must – in Newman's approach to development – therefore tend away from the truth to an ever-increasing degree. Now, the half-truth of the *via media* can be a step on the way to truth for individual believers, and indeed a 'breakwater' in the wider culture. That said, recalling moments in *Loss and Gain*, Newman's original post-conversion condemnations of the *via media* are unaffected. This is because the target of those condemnations is precisely those who mistake 'compromise' or the mean of truthfulness, for truth for its own sake: Mr Vincent is condemned because he 'had a great idea of the *via media* being the truth' and so was 'always saying things and then unsaying them', just as English pretensions about 'free thinking' are absurd when pushed to the extent they can insist that Catholicism and Protestantism are 'both right and wrong' and constitute 'two truths'.[32] Nonetheless there is a change of emphasis here – now he accepts that an Englishman can be guided 'by means' of a partial truth out of that partiality and into the fullness of truth, setting sail on the waters of the Thames, and reaching all the way to the shore of the Tiber. Nonetheless, this is a long way indeed from what John Coulson claims of the *Apologia*, as not implying

---

30. Ibid., pp. 246–7.
31. Newman, *Apologia*, pp. 326–7.
32. Newman, *Present Position*, pp. 1, 2 and 5.

'a wholesale repudiation of the [Anglican] tradition' but 'rather its affirmation in what Newman now came to regard as its legitimate setting'.[33]

9.2 System and mystery in the Grammar

A third focus to be discussed is rooted back in *Arians*, where God's mystery is a central element, pertaining particularly to God's ineffable transcendence beyond language. This dovetails comfortably with Newman's praising of English compromise for leaving many specifics of the faith 'indeterminate'. Language of mystery favours indeterminateness, which safeguards the errors the Tractarian Newman associates with overconfidently prescribing theological terrain, claiming full clarity of that which 'passeth all understanding' (Phil. 4.7). In the *Prophetical Office* 'system' is condemned as presuming to exhaust God's unplumbable depths. In the Second Spring, however, language of mystery almost entirely disappears from Newman's work, perhaps in reflection of its relation to the 'indeterminateness' granted by English compromise. Moreover, language of 'system' is rehabilitated, and an antipathy to system is even listed in *Present Position* as one of the intrinsic weaknesses of the English sensibility itself. In *Loss and Gain*, moreover, system is presented as the fruit of a sustained and deep discernment, in distinction from the superficiality of being 'viewy'. System shows the interconnection of 'fact with fact, truth with truth, the bearing of fact upon truth, and truth upon fact'. People without a system pridefully think 'they are unfettered, moderate, dispassionate' and 'observe the mean'. But rather than being 'free born Englishmen', he says, they are 'the most helpless of slaves; for our strength in this world' is to be 'captives of truth'.[34]

In the *Apologia* Newman makes a distinction between 'doubt and difficulty', which is fleshed out in much more detail when he discusses mystery in the *Essay in Aid of a Grammar of Assent* (1870). The *Grammar*'s discussion of mystery is latent in the doubt–difficulty distinction, which he makes in order to show the consistency of his thought from 1845 onwards, saying since then he has 'never have had one doubt'. He has however had difficulties, he admits, but he describes a difficulty as that which is difficult 'to imagine' but not difficult 'to believe'. A doubt is therefore that which places one's religious commitments in jeopardy. He gives the example of transubstantiation, asking 'how is it difficult to believe?' The issue is that one cannot imagine – or rather, imagistically represent in consciousness – the notion of 'substance', meaning essence, or nature. He says the substances of bread, wine, and Christ are things 'no-one on earth knows anything about', seeing only their phenomena or material appearance. He applies the same argument to the Trinity, saying the 'essence of Divine Being' (which is 'substance', again) is something he

---

33. Coulsen, *Newman and the Common Tradition*, p. 55.

34. Newman, *Loss and Gain*, pp. 16–18; see also Newman, *Idea*, p. 9, for a discussion of 'viewiness'.

cannot be expected to 'know of'. But here he introduces a second dimension of difficulty which will prove important for the *Grammar*. Not only is the notion of 'substance' impossible to imagine, there is the need to combine incompatible notions into unity. Hence, he says all he knows is that 'my abstract idea of three is simply incompatible with my idea of one'. But again, while it is difficult to conceive, it is not at all difficult to believe that 'one and three can equally be predicated of the Incommunicable God'.[35]

These two examples are utilized in the battle with Kingsley, to show that the Catholic 'system is in no sense dishonest' while leaving ample space for difficulties. More specifically, we might say here that a system which incorporates elements of mystery is not dishonest, disingenuous, nor duplicitous: it means nothing whatever like a disregarding of truth. Newman goes on, accepting difficulties, or acknowledging mystery, is not 'denying that truth is the real object of our reason' nor that having difficulties means that 'either the premise or the process is in fault'.[36] To assume the unimaginability and inconceivability of transubstantiation or the Trinity must invoke doubt rather than difficulty, is based on a faulty premise which mistakenly assumes the light of faith involves full clarity of understanding.

The difficulty regarding the mystery of the Trinity described in the *Apologia* is not so much that the human mind cannot conceive the things of God per se, but that the human mind cannot *combine* the notions involved in apprehending God, however straightforward those notions might be in and of themselves: oneness and threeness. This focus on combining notions becomes central for the account of mystery in the *Grammar*, where Newman offers a specific definition of mystery as a noetic simultaneity of notions which the human intellect cannot combine. He writes, 'A mystery is a proposition conveying incompatible notions, or is a statement of the inconceivable.' This does not threaten meaninglessness, he maintains, because we can 'assent' to mysteries 'provided we can apprehend them'. This means we can apprehend the notions we cannot combine, or the individual elements of a statement which is inconceivable when strung into a sentence. Indeed, Newman maintains that we must be able to apprehend mystery's elements, otherwise we would not know it *is* a mystery. Otherwise we would not know that it could not be known: 'Unless we comprehended it, we should not recognise it to be a mystery.'[37]

This approach to mystery is applied at length in the *Grammar*'s discussion of the Athanasian Creed. He considers this to be perfectly comprehensible in its component elements ('Father', 'Son', 'One', 'Three', etc.). The mystery is the holding of each element together in one's mind: 'combine into one, and you gain nothing but a mystery'. His metaphor of 'diffraction' is helpful for understanding the argument. We can see fragments and rays of God, but not the unified fullness of God, for that vision is granted only to 'the blessed inhabitants of heaven'. We must accept that

---

35. Newman, *Apologia*, pp. 273–4.
36. Ibid., pp. 273–5 and 277.
37. Newman, *Grammar*, pp. 43–4.

'we have but such faint reflections of It as Its diffraction supplies'.[38] This discussion makes clear a pertinent point. Newman does not simply rediscover a generalized sense of 'God as mystery' like that of *Arians*, that God is transcendent to human knowing. Rather, he offers a highly systematized approach to mystery, in which its elements are determined, and all that remains indeterminate is the combination of those elements. Here, we must part company with Walte Rost's statement that the Catholic Newman 'embodies' a 'modernist turn to indeterminacy'.[39] There is here none of that characteristic English calmness and caution, no celebration of compromise as leaving space for unutterable nature of God. Indeed, as Clyde Nabe points out, Newman is explicit that even God himself is not a mystery *in se*. It 'is the nature of the human intellect which brings us face to face with mystery', not something which belongs to what Newman calls 'the Divine Verity as such'.[40] This distinction is often lost by those who too quickly apportion a later understanding of mystery to Newman, including Connolly who inaccurately glosses Newman's position by saying we 'cannot have a real apprehension of the Trinity as a whole because of the mystery of God'.[41] It is rather because of the limits of the internal structuring, the grammar, of human apprehension.

The unsystematic and indeterminate theology praised by the Tractarian Newman stands equally condemned during the Second Spring and the mature writings, therefore. In the *Present Position*, Newman states that 'certain peculiarities of the English character' are displayed in Anglicanism, particularly the Englishness of being indisposed to the system. He says Catholic theologians 'view Catholic truth as a whole, as one great system of which part grows out of part, and doctrine corresponds to doctrine' and they 'carry out' their doctrinal 'system' into 'its fulness'. But this is 'distasteful to an Englishman', for 'we ourselves ... break away' from it as 'dry' and 'theoretical'.[42] Newman's mature theology of mystery is no rediscovery of his earlier work. Mystery in the *Grammar* is theoretical enough to remain as distasteful to the Englishman as any Catholic system, there is no compromise here.

9.3 Freeborn subjects of the pope

The third focus for this discussion is the papal infallibility controversy. Newman's moderate approach to papal infallibility is commonly presented as constituting

---

38. Ibid., p. 128.

39. Walter Jost, *Rhetorical Thought in John Henry Newman* (South Carolina: University of South Carolina Press, 1989), p. xi.

40. Clyde Nabe, *Mystery and Religion: Newman's Epistemology of Religion* (Lanham, MD: University Press of America, 1988), p. 16.

41. John R. Connolly, *John Henry Newman: A View of Catholic Faith for the New Millennium* (Lanham, MD: Rowland and Littlefield, 2005), p. 122.

42. Newman, *Present Position*, p. 57.

some sort of Catholic *via media*. Stephen Thomas argues that Newman 'found himself to be a liberal within Roman Catholicism' with this controversy.[43] James Cameron suggests Newman's 'coolness to ultramontane theology' was 'formed on the Tractarian mould'.[44] Chadwick describes the controversy with marked implications related to the *via media*, saying Newman 'denounced Roman Catholic extremists' who 'treated' every 'moderate' position as 'disloyal to the Pope'.[45] Avery Dulles suggests that Newman remained 'an apostle of the *via media*' throughout his life, with the infallibility controversy presenting a middle path between 'Gallicanism and ultramontanism', and Ker similarly argues that his position is a *via media* between 'restorationists' and 'modernizers'.[46]

It is easy enough to understand how the proposal solemnly to define papal infallibility was so problematic for those caught up in the English sensibility. As put by Newman in the *Present Position*, the 'great mass of educated men' consider it fitting to 'their Christian liberty' to have such 'freedom of choice of essentials of the faith'.[47] The popular mind of England considered this freedom to be irreconcilable with the notion of papal infallibility which was discussed in the run-up to the formal definition of such at the Vatican Council of 1869–70.

Newman was deeply uncomfortable during the prior discussions of the definition, or rather uncomfortable about how broad some of his co-religionists wanted the definition to be. Newman considered calls for a definition to be a development not adequately prepared for, or lacking sufficient grounds, in the tradition. Newman also had further reservations surrounding the need for a definition, insofar as there was no heresy to correct, there were no Catholics threatening schism over the issue (at least until the definition was promulgated, ironically).[48] Following the publication of the definition, Newman wrote of his relief and joy that it was suitably 'moderate', and avoided the neo-ultramontane desire for an extension of infallibility to the realm of temporal power and not just faith and morals,[49] although he does not mention the opposing Gallican extreme.

Newman's position towards the definition is expounded fully in his *Letter to the Duke of Norfolk*. The text itself gives little evidence of a desire to moderate between extremes. His opening discussion of the Irish bishops implies that their error was, to Newman's mind, the same as the Anglican's: 'Ireland is not the only country in which politics, or patriotism' has 'been so closely associated with religion in the

---

43. Stephen Thomas, *Newman and Heresy: The Anglican Years*, p. 5.
44. Cameron in introduction to *Development*, p. 25.
45. Chadwick, *Newman*, pp. 67–8. Chadwick argues that Newman set out to 'weaken extremists', heavily implying reminiscences of the *via media*.
46. Avery Dulles S. J. 'Newman on Infallibility', *Theological Studies*, vol. 51 (1990) and Ker, *Newman and Vatican II*, p. 76.
47. Newman, *Present Position*, p. 57.
48. See Ker, *Newman*, pp. 651–5.
49. Ibid., 655 and Newman, *Letters and Diaries Volume XXV*, p. 161.

nation ... that it is difficult to say which' is 'uppermost'.[50] The ensuing argument is, by his own description, not concerned with theology but only 'secular discourse between England and Rome'.[51] Nonetheless, he states in a discussion of Erastianism that the Church must be either 'independent of the state' or a subject of it, and 'there was no middle term'.[52] The main force of his ire is towards the defenders of the old English affection for free thinking, for the moderation of *audi alteram partem*, especially William Gladstone. These were those who ever saw Catholics as 'moral and mental slaves' for whom the pope's awesome power must surely 'try the temper of a free-born Englishman'.[53] He remains as invective as he was in his satires to those who extend 'English liberty of speech' and 'the press' to liberty of 'worship'.[54]

The point most salient for this discussion is that, when Newman claims 'I see no inconsistency in my being at once a good Catholic and a good Englishman', he is not referring to a general commitment to seeking a middle path, to 'moderation in all things'. Neither is he claiming that the English settlement somehow aligns with a position which balances Gallicanism and ultramontanism. Rather, he is holding that the formal definition itself does not inherently conflict with the domain of secular law, to things 'accidental, changeable, and of mere expedience'.[55] Any middle path between those calling for extreme over- or understatements of papal infallibility, then, is restricted to the case at hand and in no way constitutes a Catholic variant of his earlier commitments.

9.4 Summary

The overall impression given by the foci of this chapter is that the aspect of the English sensibility under discussion here – compromise – remains, as in the Second Spring, like 'the paganism of old' to have been 'shattered into pieces by the unassailable march of the truth'. This is shown by Newman's mature description of the event of 1841, which maintains all the commitments of the earlier description in *Difficulties*. Truth is not a virtue, again, strictly speaking, it is not arrived at by mediating between extremes. The same applies to the discussion of 'mystery' in the *Grammar*, which is a deeply determinate and systematic treatment of this topic. The same broad principle applies again to the papal infallibility controversy, suggesting that calling this a 'Catholic *via media*' is to overstate the case if that is

---

50. John Henry Newman, *A Letter Addressed to the Duke of Norfolk on Occasion of Mr. Gladstone's Recent Expostulation: Certain Difficulties Felt by Anglicans in Catholic Teaching Volume 2* (New York: Longmans, Green, 1900), p. 185.
51. Ibid., p. 186.
52. Ibid., p. 200.
53. Ibid., pp. 224 and 227.
54. Ibid., p. 271.
55. Ibid., p. 231.

taken as a resurgent Englishness at work in Newman's Catholic life. The nearest we get to a rapprochement here is in the more conciliatory statements about Anglicanism we read in the *Apologia*. But, even here, while the half-truth of the *via media* can be a step on the way to truth for individual believers and a 'breakwater' in the wider culture, the most that can be hoped is that one might get 'guidance by means of it out of it'.[56]

The previous discussion of compromise in Newman's Second Spring writings left this attribute of an English sensibility firmly on the side of nature, with nature being rooted in the interplay of human life and a particular locality, natural attributes pertaining to particular peoples cannot be raised to universal provenance. The overarching sense of this chapter is that this remains unchanged for the mature Newman. Englishness is a flowering of nature, which must never be confused with grace. While it need not always lead away from God – and one might get 'guidance by means of it out of it' – one still needs to get out of it if one is to encounter that which is genuinely and fully true. At best, Englishness can lead a horse to the living water, but it can never make the horse drink of it, for that impulse is granted by God alone.

---

56. Newman, *Apologia*, pp. 246–7.

Chapter 10

RESERVE IN THE MATURE NEWMAN

We have seen reserve plays a key part in Newman's earliest work *Arians* and is a key feature of Tractarianism generally. In *Arians* this takes shape by Newman's drawing of analogies between the Alexandrian scheme of initiation and Christian life more broadly. In Alexandria the reserve with which dogmatic formulae are treated was something to be progressed beyond by virtue of baptism, rather than a permanent feature of Christian life *tout court*. During the Second Spring period, however, Newman's attitude to reserve undergoes significant change, centred on his utilization of the supernatural virtue of faith in *Difficulties*. There, the lack of reserve he observes in Catholic populations is indicative of a great spiritual gift, for those bearing this gift speak of divine things freely, if profanely. The Alexandrian scheme has fallen out of view in *Difficulties*: those with the supernatural virtue of faith can know divine things without their affections being cultivated beforehand. That said, however, a question remains as to how supernatural grace might pertain in those who are not profane, or how the affections can be cultivated on the basis of grace.

The second difficulty is that, while the Catholic 'multitude' exhibit their receipt of the great spiritual benefit of faith in *Difficulties*, in his earlier discussions of formal theology in the *Development* essay, Newman holds firm to his reserve about language in relation to dogma. If the Catholic masses have a supernatural virtue which allows them to speak of divine things as freely as the English might speak of 'railroads and electric telegrams', does this not threaten to contradict statements from *Development*, such as: 'creeds and dogmas are necessary only because the human mind cannot reflect' on the Divine Nature?[1] Related to this view of dogma as necessary but unfortunate is the point noted in my reading of *Arians*, that the creeds have ever been put to use in liturgical settings, often with a reverence and enthusiasm which suggests they are a cause for celebration, not unfortunate necessities. Here, we have a specific and technical outworking of Newman's struggles with the English sensibility in collision with Catholicism, as if a reassessment of the habits of mind of the multitude cannot be harmonized with the residual sense of reserve apportioned to dogma. The question is, then,

---

1. Newman, *Development*, pp. 114–16.

whether reserve will, like compromise, keep Englishness firmly on the 'natural' side of things, or show itself as something capable of gracious elevation.

10.1 Affections and passions

10.1.1 Affections and passions in the Apologia

This section will interrogate Newman's mature writings to inquire as to whether the omission of the possibility of a graced cultivation of the affections is answered there. This requires an extensive discussion of the *Grammar* in the following subsection, but here I want to draw attention to how reserve occasionally crops up in the *Apologia*. Firstly, Kingsley's charge of dishonesty is made against Newman in relation both to an apparent lack of reserve in Newman's own writing and preaching, and also for Newman's use *of* reserve, as 'economy'. In the first case, Kingsley criticizes *Difficulties* for its 'subtle paradoxes' and 'rhetorical exaggerations' when 'truth and honesty' are discussed therein. Kingsley claims that Newman takes 'a perverse pleasure' in 'saying something shocking to plain English notions'. As regards the doctrine of 'economy', it is easy to discern how this would provide ample fuel for Kingsley to accuse Newman of deliberate deceit. Newman responds by seeking to delimit the domain of 'reserve and economy' in such a way that Kingsley's accusation does not hold. He does however concede that a revision of his view of St Clement of Alexandria was required, insofar as he now agrees with those who say the saint does indeed permit lying in the service of the truth, whereas the young Newman thought 'he used the word "lie" as hyperbole'.[2]

Interestingly, there are two points in the *Apologia* where the issues at stake in this chapter are intensified. The first is shown by Kingsley's shock at Newman's claim in *Difficulties* that 'a mere beggar woman' who 'is not over-scrupulous of truth' will 'in the eyes of the Church, have a prospect of heaven quite closed and refused to the State's pattern-man' no matter how 'honourable' and 'conscientious' he might be, if his honour comes 'not from a supernatural power, but from a mere natural virtue'.[3] These comments are a demonstration of Newman's point about the supernatural virtue of faith as distinct from truthfulness as a natural virtue, but an important possibility arises here, namely omission from the Second Spring period: the possibility of there being a third example, someone with genteel affections and passions grounded in grace. How might an affection and desire for truthfulness or honour develop on the basis of a supernatural gift, coming 'from a supernatural power'? The 'State's pattern-man' has naturally cultivated affections and passions, the 'beggar woman' is profane in worldly terms but inestimably rich in grace.

The second point of intensification comes with some observations Newman shares shortly after defending his earlier adoption of 'economy'. He writes, 'When

---

2. Newman, *Apologia*, p. 297.
3. Ibid., p. 41.

I became a Catholic, nothing struck me more at once than the English out-spoken manner of the Priests.' He notes this was the same Oscott, Old Hall Green, and Ushaw, where Catholic clergy were 'more natural and unaffected than many an English clergyman'. This challenges the prejudiced conceptions of Catholic priests as having 'smoothness' and 'mannerism'. What is implied in these remarks is again the cultivation of affections without grace – decorum, reserve, discretion construed in merely worldly terms. These are 'manners' like Burke's, but they 'vex' rather than 'sooth', while aiming to do the latter. Much the same point relates to Newman's disdain for the Anglican 'parsonic voice', a style of vocal expression different from normal, everyday speech.[4] Such affected decorum aligns with the 'pattern-man's' honour and conscientiousness. That is, it is a merely aesthetic cultivation of the self not grounded in 'supernatural power', and thus not integral to the whole person, so feels affected and insincere.

10.1.2 Affections and passions in the Grammar

In the *Grammar* Newman provides the technical detail for understanding the cultivation of the affections on the basis of supernatural faith, which is lacking in both the beggar woman and parsonically voiced Anglican clergy. To give an overview of the book itself, it would today perhaps best be classified as 'philosophical theology'. The *Grammar*'s focus is on asking how believing or 'assent' arises in the phenomena of empirical consciousness, and with describing the internal structure or 'grammar' of such acts of assent in that consciousness.[5] While it would be anachronistic to call the book 'phenomenological', many commentators have pointed to various ways in which Newman's approach prefigures important developments in later continental thought.[6] That said, the book has had a mixed reception, and remains woefully unread compared to other works of the corpus. It is however a crucial work for understanding the whole

---

4. Ian Ker, *The Catholic Revival in English Literature 1845–1961* (London: Gracewing, 2003).

5. This view concurs with Walgrave, *Newman*, p. 62, but not Jay Newman, who argues in *The Mental Philosophy of John Henry Newman* (Ontario: Wilfred Laurier University Press, 1986) that the word 'grammar' also 'signals the books concern with language', p. 15.

6. See Thomas K. Carr, *Newman and Gadamer: Toward a Hermeneutics of Religious Knowledge* (Oxford: Oxford University Press, 1996), and Jay Newman, *Mental Philosophy*, pp. 9 and 23–5; H. P. Owen compares him to Kant, in *The Moral Argument for Christian Theism* (London: Allen & Unwin, 1965), p. 7; both O'Donoghue, in 'Privileged Access' (p. 243), and Coplestone, *A History of Philosophy Volume 8: 2* (London: Continuum, 2003) (p. 287) to Kierkegaard, Cronin in *Knowledge* (pp. 129–36) and Hollis, *World* (pp. 166–7) to Bergson, Norris *Method* and Ferreira *Doubt* (p. 38) to Polanyi. Others consider Newman to be closer to intellectual movements contemporary with his life, for example, Goslee's claim that his writings are 'complicit with a deeper, intellectual and emotional current flourishing from English and German Romanticism', in *Romanticism and the Anglican Newman* (Ohio: Ohio University Press, 1996), p. 3.

oeuvre, not least because it is, as put by John R. Connolly, the 'major source for Newman's mature understanding of Catholic faith'.[7] Indeed, Jay Newman goes further, calling it 'an attempt at self-vindication' because it seeks to expound his epistemology in such a way as to 'persuade his Roman Catholic superiors that he is not nearly as unorthodox and untrustworthy as many of his Catholic critics have repeatedly insisted'.[8]

Newman's first step is to show that assent is in itself a distinct act of consciousness, not conditional upon preliminary steps, although such steps nearly always precede it. This contradicts what Newman calls the 'rationalist' view, that assent is or can or should only be granted when the person assenting is satisfied as to the cogency of the inferences which precede it. Newman argues against rationalism by pointing out that assent does not always require inferences, strictly speaking. People frequently assent to a great many things without needing to infer as to the rectitude of that assent, although they often cast their minds back and establish what the criteria for the assent were, retrospectively. Moreover, people frequently assent to things in life for which the phenomena of consciousness are far too many and far too complex to delineate into the premises of formal logic, even if one wished to. In decision-making, the one assenting does so 'by a mental comprehension of the whole case' and often 'by a clear and rapid act of the intellect' involving an unreflective 'unwritten summing-up' enabling the individual to decide this way or that.[9]

The *Grammar* analyses, in considerable detail, the various phenomena making up all acts of assent with a view to showing that lived human ratiocination is more fundamentally about this last sort of unreflective 'assent', than the premises and conclusions of 'formal logic' used in 'argumentative science'. Newman points out that a 'mental comprehension', a 'whole case' which is far too vast and complex to be distilled into formal premises, can still be considered and painstaking; it is just that the mind does not proceed by way of certain premises or singular terms, let alone formal inference. People 'sense' or 'intuit' their way through complex circumstances. Formal logic simply cannot capture it, but it is in no way irrational.

Newman thus launches his most extensive critique against that rationalism which was increasing in influence in the nineteenth century. He seeks to broaden the received scope of 'ratiocination' so it encompasses both 'the exercise of a living faculty' in 'concrete life' as well as 'formal logic' and 'skill in argumentative science'.[10] His early steps in working towards this involve some highly original epistemic insights, such as the distinction between 'notional' and 'real' apprehension. He states that in apprehending propositions, the terms might either 'stand for things', which are then 'singular nouns' coming 'from experience', or they 'stand for

---

7. Connolly, *John Henry Newman*, p. 32.
8. Newman, *Mental Philosophy*, pp. 18–19.
9. Newman, *Grammar*, pp. 284–5.
10. Ibid., p. 295.

notions' which are then 'common nouns' coming 'from abstraction'.[11] The two forms of apprehension are of course very often combined; there is frequently no 'line of demarcation or party-wall' between the two.[12] This can be seen with the example of apprehending the proposition 'a mother loves her child'. As notional, it is a general principle pertaining to the notions of mother and offspring. As 'real' it refers to concrete individuals in experience. The differing emphases between the notional and the real will vary in considerable degree according to context, being particularly 'real' when glancing at a photograph of oneself in one's mother's arms, for example, compared with its use as a premise in a deductive syllogism, say. Sometimes apprehension also moves from the predominantly 'real' to being predominantly 'notional'. Interestingly, Newman gives an example of this with propositions about 'national character', as when the 'real' basis of propositions 'almost' ceases to play any role for it is just assumed as a stereotype. Then, he writes, one expects 'cold and selfish Scots, crafty Italians, vulgar Americans and Frenchmen, [as] half-tiger, half monkey'. The point is that these expectations hold as mere notions, although Newman assumes they once arose from the behaviour of concretely existing ('real') individuals. Hence, Newman mentions that people are surprised at meeting a Frenchman who was 'tall and stout, because it was the received idea that all Frenchmen were under-sized and lived on frogs'.[13]

Newman proceeds to put the two forms of apprehension to use to describe correspondingly 'real' or 'notional' assents, that is, for example, in agreeing that 'a mother loves her child' in different contexts like those mentioned above. This enables Newman to work towards his aim of describing the breadth of the reasoning of the 'living intellect' in 'concrete life'. This breadth is shown in that formal inference pertains only to assents involving predominately notional apprehension. This serves to broaden the parameters of reasoning beyond mere logic, because Newman maintains that the 'normal' occurrence of assent comes from apprehending 'things', and is thus 'real'. We are reasoning about things countless times throughout each day, and only comparatively rarely about notions, that is, about 'abstract nouns'.[14]

Yet there is more than a mere frequency of occurrence at stake here. Real assents are primary over notional because of their affect on life, that is, their urgency, their importance, and their intensity. This is because 'what is concrete exerts a force and makes an impression on the mind which nothing abstract can rival'. It is 'in human nature to be more affected by the concrete than by the abstract'.[15] In notional assent, the components of deliberation are the mind's 'own creations' – that is, ideas, or concepts, and so on. In real assent, the mind is directed 'toward things' and these impose on our deliberations and decisions differently to purely

---

11. Ibid., p. 20.
12. Ibid., p. 95.
13. Ibid., p. 30.
14. Ibid., p. 35.
15. Ibid.

noetic phenomena. Newman argues that the things of life impose themselves on consciousness as images, which are 'the impressions' things leave 'on the imagination'.[16] Great swathes of the activity of human ratiocination, as it occurs in concrete life, are therefore imagistic rather than syllogistic. This means our imaginations are bound up with reason, with the way we assent in concrete life.

This brings us back to the affections and passions. Our affections and passions are seen by Newman as 'aroused' by the imagination, not by the intellect cogitating notions. He writes that real assents are 'the more vivid and forcible' and so 'intellectual ideas cannot compete in effectiveness with the experience of concrete life'.[17] By 'effectiveness', Newman means real assents become 'motive causes' for action. This is not because 'real apprehension, as such, impels to action' but because 'it excites and stimulates the affections and passions, by bringing facts home to them as motive causes'.[18] Therefore, 'images' have 'an influence both on the individual and on society, which mere notions cannot exert'.[19] To restate the point, imagination itself does not cause action, it stimulates desires (or passions), by 'providing a supply of objects strong enough to stimulate them'.[20] In short, we respond desirously to images but not to concepts, so Jost is right when he calls Newman's understanding of the imagination 'affective'.[21] In this connection we can quote some of Newman's most oft-repeated epithets like 'it is the concrete being that reasons', and indeed the motto on the frontispiece of the *Grammar* itself: 'Non in dialectica complacuit Deo Salvum facere populum suum'.

Now, it is relatively self-evident from the foregoing that Newman's discussion of the supernatural virtue of faith in *Difficulties* strongly suggests that the 'vivid perception, like sense, of things unseen' he there describes pertains to real apprehension and assent.[22] Indeed, Newman makes this link more or less explicit in a reversed form, when he discusses an English proclivity towards notional apprehension in religious matters. Having distinguished religion as pertaining to real assent, and theology to the notional, Newman highlights a notional peculiarity as the dominant English variant of Christianity. He argues that *religion* itself is often approached as notional by the English. Religion, he claims, 'should be real' but 'is commonly not real in England'. He has in mind particularly the so-called 'Bible Religion' of popular Protestantism. This is confusing, because we would expect a biblical faith to be intensely imagistic. Nonetheless, Newman maintains

---

16. Ibid., p. 72.
17. Ibid., pp. 9–10.
18. Ibid.
19. Ibid.
20. Ibid., p. 79.
21. Jost in *Rhetorical Thought* points to this as one of two aspects of imagination in Newman, that is, what he calls their 'affectivity' but also their 'polysemousness' because then 'the concrete' that is imaged 'forth is itself determinable only within the broader horizon of interpretation postulated by the inquirer', p. 152.
22. Newman, *Difficulties*, pp. 273–4.

that English 'Bible Religion' is a religion not 'of persons and things, of acts of faith', nor 'of direct devotion', because its 'doctrines are not so much facts, as stereotypical aspects of facts'.[23] The point here seems to be that the English popular mind is not aroused by the dramas and stories of the Bible but rigidly binds its 'sacred scenes' to demonstrative principles for 'living a correct life', so this Bible Religion is 'at best notional'.[24]

Such is of course not the case in Catholic countries, however. Newman writes in a way markedly reminiscent of his discussion of the supernatural virtue of faith in *Difficulties* when he states that for 'Catholic populations', by contrast with the English, 'assent to religious objects is real, not notional'. To such people, we read, 'the Supreme Being, our Lord, the Blessed Virgin, Angels and Saints, heaven and hell, are as present as if they are objects of sight', recalling his comments in *Difficulties* about their 'vivid perception, like sense, of things unseen'.[25]

These resonances between real apprehension and assent in the *Grammar*, and the supernatural virtue of faith in *Difficulties*, provide an opportunity to highlight the cohesiveness and consistency of Newman's mature thought. Recall that as far back as 1828 he had presented affections and passions as primary: 'words are not feelings' and 'intellect seems to be but the attendant and servant of right feeling'.[26] In *Arians*, moreover, he says the object of 'religious veneration' is 'unseen, and dissimilar from all that is seen', and so our representations of it 'should ever be subordinate to the cultivation of religious affections'.[27] During the Second Spring period, however, he argues that Catholics are in receipt of a supernatural virtue which gives them the power as good as sight of divine things, regardless of the uncultivated state of their affections and passions. Indeed, cultivated affections themselves are treated with suspicion, as with 'the State's pattern-man'. Added to this, there are Newman's statements in the *Grammar* which seem to contradict those of his salad days, like 'knowledge must ever precede the exercise of the affections', and 'in religion the imagination and affections should always be under the control of reason'.[28]

The system of the *Grammar* enables us to integrate the factors at play. In *Arians* reserve is necessary in order to ensure the affections are cultivated prior to the disclosure of divine things. In *Difficulties* reserve is no longer necessary at all, and

---

23. Newman, *Grammar*, pp. 54–5.
24. Ibid., p. 55.
25. Ibid., p. 53 and Newman, *Difficulties*, pp. 273–4. It could be argued that Newman does not mention 'faith' in this discussion, which is indeed correct. However, he does enter into the somewhat vexed question of how the cognition of faith relates to worldly cognition elsewhere in the book.
26. Newman, *Letters & Diaries Volume I*, p. 60. See also a letter to Mrs Newman: 'words are poor to express completed feelings on many occasions' (p. 145), and to Francis Newman 'I give no credit to *words*' (p. 183).
27. Newman, *Arians*, p. 143.
28. Newman, *Grammar*, p. 98.

those without the discretion of reserve are indeed often closer to the things of God than the cultivated gentleman. In the *Grammar*, we finally see how the affections can be cultivated aright, if that is done *on the basis* of a real assent to divine things. The uncultivated beggar woman remains nearer to God than even the most cultivated 'pattern man' who dines every evening at high table, for she assents with real assent. Yet a crucial new element comes into play here: an understanding of the cultivated affections on the basis of a genuine ('real') assent or faith. While the affections are stimulated as 'motive powers' by the 'objects of the imagination', that passion stimulated in faith can and often does take shape in ways which reflect and mirror the cultural sensibilities of the believer. The key thing is to ensure that those sensibilities do not negate or undermine the original, supernatural impetus.[29]

On this front, we glimpse something of what it might mean for Newman to consider someone a Catholic, English gentleman. His discussions from the *Idea* being close to the point, 'the "gentleman" is the creation, not of Christianity, but of civilisation' because 'the Church aims at regenerating the very depths of the heart', most obviously perhaps with the supernatural virtue of faith.[30] The gentleman is at this stage described as 'the beau-ideal of the world' whose 'lineaments … partly assist and partly distort the development of a Catholic'.[31] But now we can understand the assistance of a cultivated or civilized nature to a person reborn by grace. The point is made, in an inverted fashion, by some of Newman's mature comments about Marian devotion. Whereas a sermon from the Second Spring period connected English reservations with a 'deficiency' – or what the *Idea* calls the 'distortion' of Catholic development – the mature Newman accepts those reservations. In the *Apologia* he writes that 'such passages as are found in the works of Italian authors' are 'not acceptable to every part of the Catholic world'. This is not because they are wrong, let alone heretical, it is because their rectitude cannot be lifted beyond the notional. They 'may be explained and defended; but sentiment and taste do not run with logic'. So Newman concludes, 'they are suitable for Italy, but they are not for suitable for England'.[32] The point is that suitability remains important, even when grounded on faith.

As put in his response to Pusey's *Eirenicon*, the 'forced style' of Italian and Spanish devotion 'would simply be unintelligible' in England. He concludes that if 'the Catholic faith spreads in England' believers will be able 'to love her as a Mother, to honour her as a Virgin, to seek her as a Patron, and to exalt her as a Queen, without any injury to solid piety and Christian good sense' and this reserved approach – informed by national sensibilities – he says 'I cannot help' calling 'the English style'.[33] This is not, as Cameron says, indicative of 'Newman's steadfast opposition to the Italianate devotions' as if that were evidence of an

---

29. Newman, *Grammar*, p. 79.
30. Newman, *Idea*, p. 142.
31. Ibid., p. 147.
32. Newman, *Apologia*, p. 238.
33. Ibid., p. 100.

enduring 'Tractarian spirit'.³⁴ Neither is it aligned to Chadwick's comment that Newman 'threw overboard an excess of adulation of St Mary'.³⁵ It is rather that Newman reaches a point where there can be an influence of national sensibility 'after' one is reborn in grace, by faith – there is no such a thing as an 'English style', if it remains merely 'style' and never substance – at the level of which such devotions 'can be explained and defended'.

10.2 Dogmatic formulations as positive in the Grammar

As stated at the outset of this chapter, Newman seems to remain committed to his reserved view of dogma from *Arians* in his Second Spring period, to the degree that he seems inconsistent. The supernatural virtue of faith is not applied to the imagery and allusions of the creeds, so there is no possibility of credal doxology nor *kataphasis*. Here again we find in the *Grammar*, however, a point where this tension is ironed out, and Newman's theology is integrated.

The point at issue begins with Newman pointing out that the language of dogma can stand for a 'notion or a thing', meaning it can be assented to notionally or real-ly. He says that a real assent 'is an act of religion' whereas a notional assent 'is a theological act'. The former assents to a 'realty' apprehended by the 'imagination', the second to 'a truth' apprehended by the 'intellect'.³⁶ It might be tempting here to think this means Newman's view from *Arians* – that dogma is necessary but unfortunate – applies to the notional side, insofar as intellectual scrutiny can hardly be avoided but is not without threat to devotional fervour. Newman does not decide this, however. It will be recalled that the real and the notional are ever mixed up in concrete life, there is 'no line of demarcation' between 'these two modes of assent', he says. Therefore he will not accept there could be an 'antagonism between a dogmatic and a vital religion'.³⁷ The vital religion, real assent, is binding on all. Focusing on 'intellectual notions' is not necessary, as such, real assent is imperative on both the 'learned and unlearned'. But this does not mean the full power of the intellectual is irrelevant, far from it. Indeed, there are times when 'vital religion' requires it, in just the same way 'language is ever necessary for denoting facts'.³⁸ This is because faith issues in devotion through the affections, but the affections can dry up and even believers run into difficulties while believing. Then 'sentiment … falls back upon the intellect for its stay', and 'devotion falls back upon dogma'.³⁹ We might phrase this differently by saying supernature falls back on nature, faith

---

34. Cameron in introduction to Newman, *Development*, p. 25.
35. Chadwick, *Newman*, pp. 65–6.
36. Newman, *Grammar*, p. 95.
37. Ibid., pp. 95 and 98.
38. Ibid., p. 98.
39. Ibid.

falls back on reason – or rather reason bolsters and revivifies the life of faith even if at first it seemed a total break from it.

It is this insight about the inseparability of 'vital' and 'intellectual' religion for a mature life of faith that allows Newman finally to connect credal statements of belief with doxology. He reminds us that the Athanasian Creed was called the *Psalmus Quicunque* in the early Church, and is thus not 'a mere collection of notions' but a 'psalm or hymn of praise'. The interrelation of real and notional, vital and intellectual, is signified by the ancient rule, '*lex orandi, lex credendi*'.[40] As put by Ker, we have indeed 'come a long way from *The Arians*, where dogma was seen as hardly more than a necessary evil, to a position where doctrinal formulations are viewed as indispensable for personal faith'. Here, dogma does not just protect 'religion from error, but doctrinal propositions are now viewed as integral to faith itself'.[41] A reserve rooted in a suspicion of language is still here, insofar as an intellectual or notional religion is insufficient in that it is a mere 'matter of words or logic instead of having its seat in the heart'.[42] But now that reserve can be graciously elevated and put in service of grace itself.[43]

10.3 Summary

The question this chapter seeks to answer is: whether reserve will, like compromise, keep Englishness firmly on the 'natural' side of things, or show itself as something capable of gracious elevation. In the first place, there is a significant shift here insofar as Newman's mature writings on the affections provide the detail for understanding how this aspect of the English sensibility can be incorporated with Catholicism. The latter serves as the ground or basis, of course – there must be real assent – but secondary to that a richly desiring life can be portrayed and expressed in ways which would be deemed intrinsically English.

The same is true of regarding Newman's revised position towards dogma being necessary but unfortunate. Here, we have a specific and technical outworking of Newman's struggles with the English sensibility in collision with Catholicism. A reserve rooted in the suspicion of language is still present in the *Grammar*. But now that reserve is graciously elevated and put in service of the supernatural,

---

40. Ibid., pp. 128–9.
41. Ian Ker, *Newman on Being a Christian* (South Bend: Notre Dame University Press, 1990).
42. Newman, *Grammar*, p. 98.
43. See Newman, *Letters and Diaries Volume LDXXIII*

> Does not mean that it is possible, or even desirable, to list all the doctrines which a Catholic at any given time has to believe … The Catholic position is that 'the object of faith is not simple certain articles … contained in the dumb documents, but the whole word of God, explicit and implicit, as dispensed by His living Church'. (pp. 99–100)

while never being based on language, on what Newman calls 'dumb documents', even the supernatural life of faith must sometimes make recourse back to the notional in order to stay vital and living. Interestingly, this second point is hardly distinctively English, although it is distinctively Newmanian. Perhaps this suggests it is particularly important. Here we can discern how the struggles with and within a particular sensibility arrive at a point of universal insight, the particular becomes inextricable from the universal.

Chapter 11

EMPIRICISM IN THE MATURE NEWMAN

The discussion of empiricism so far found that the Tractarian Newman firstly evinces a markedly empirical prioritizing of action over ideas, seen particularly in the *Parochial and Plain Sermons*. Secondly and conversely, there is Newman's willingness to deviate from the traditional principles of 'pragmatism', through attempts to bring 'an assemblage of words' hitherto under the province of 'reason' (the *via media*), to bear on the Church of England, which challenges a particular aspect of English empiricism.

Newman of the Second Spring, however, seems almost to forgo his empiricism. He ferociously critiques popular understandings of an empirical mindset, in relation to the Industrial Revolution and the legal, parliamentarian tradition. The *Development* essay is an exception, having a marked empirical focus. But this text was written while Newman was still Anglican, and it is also important to bear in mind that in the *Present Position* even the study of empirical history itself is presented as un-English. This discussion was left, therefore, with English empiricism seeming to be left behind. The Second Spring sermon itself, after all, describes the irruption of Catholicism onto the land of England as a miraculous intervention which sharply contradicts usual patterns of empirical development. This chapter will seek to discern how empiricism is at play in the mature Newman, with a view to establishing if it remains peripheral for his Catholic writings, or is rediscovered and integrated with the work of the Second Spring.

11.1 The illative sense

A curious feature of Newman's apparent forsaking of his empiricism in the Second Spring period arises through his description of English empiricism as inimical to the study of history. As we have seen, in the *Present Position* he highlights English antipathies to 'system' and 'fact', and the latter is particularly surprising given the received notion (often acknowledged by Newman himself) of English empiricism as prioritizing fact over idea. Yet, Newman maintains that 'an Englishman' takes 'little interest' in 'past times and foreign countries', and is therefore 'apathetic to historical fact'.[1] Recalling that Newman's own empirical commitments ground the methodology of his historical survey of Christian antiquity in the *Development* essay, there seems to be a tension between Newman and Englishness here. That is, *Development* is either not empirical in any English way, or the method he utilizes in *Development* is different from the tendencies he critiques in the *Present Position*.

Returning to the *Grammar* provides the means by which the second of these options is proved correct. Newman's means of argumentation in *Development* are not straightforward historical study as such. He does not begin with particular findings and sources, in fact he makes precious little reference to sources at all. Rather, he works from empirical *consciousness*, beginning his inquiry with the process by which human minds make 'habitual judgements' about 'the things that come before them', which form into developing constellations of judgements which can be said to reflect 'ideas'. Moreover, Newman does not only use human consciousness as his point of departure, he also works with the Church as a present fact which is known through the impressions given to empirical consciousness. Newman works with 'facts': the fact of the existing Church as our most 'natural informant' as to what Christianity is, and more broadly the 'fact' of empirical consciousness itself.

The *Grammar* itself distinguishes between these different meanings of 'fact', and this is important, I suggest, because he now utilizes his empirical method (focused on facts of consciousness) to show how empiricism could actually lead people *to* Catholic truth. After all, the *Grammar*'s empirical orientation is hard to overstate. Newman describes his concern with processes like apprehending, assenting, inferring, and so on, as pertaining only to 'their bearing upon concrete matter', meaning our 'experience of concrete facts'.[2] He is not therefore concerned with concepts, as such, except insofar as these apply to 'the experience of human life, as it is daily brought before us'.[3] He considers 'formal logic' vastly overrepresented because it leads to a view of human decision-making as mere 'abstraction' and not effectively 'carried into the realities of life'.[4] Moreover, to reduce 'assent' to the methods of 'argumentative science' means we never reach the human being 'as a concrete fact'.[5] References such as these – all focused on 'the facts of human nature, as they are found in the concrete action of life' – show that the method of descriptive psychology first begun in the opening pages of the *Development* essay is here extended into a more far-reaching endeavour.[6] In the earlier work, it served to illustrate how the mind gets to grips with the idea of Christianity, and how that idea develops through time in such a way as to remain tethered to the original referent. Now, the descriptive method is used to illustrate not only

---

1. Newman, *Present Position*, pp. 57–63.
2. Newman, *Grammar*, pp. 5 and 9–10.
3. Ibid., p. 158.
4. Ibid., p. 286.
5. Ibid., p. 281.
6. Ibid., p. 168.

doctrinal development but also wide-ranging features of human psychology, with foundational consequences that challenge dominant assumptions about the structure of human knowledge itself.

The *Grammar*'s conclusion is what Newman calls 'the illative sense', drawn from the noun illation, which is derived from the past participle of the Latin for 'to infer', *inferre*, which is *illatus*. Literally, the illative sense is, then, an 'inferred' sense. The past tense indicates that it involves judgements about a matter at hand, about which a multitude of judgements have already occurred as the matter is brought to consciousness. But these preliminary or constitutive prior judgements are not inferences in the formal sense, not a breaking down into components then constructed into premises. They are described by Newman as 'informal inferences'. As we have seen, he maintains that in all manner of everyday decisions a vast number of implicit inferences are operating, more than could ever be consciously ascertained and listed for the purpose of formal deliberation. As he writes, they are 'too fine to avail separately, too subtle and circuitous to be convertible into syllogisms, too numerous and various for such conversion, even were they convertible'.[7]

Informal inferences differ not only from the premises of formal logic in their subtlety and volume but also in their particular type of certainty. The seemingly limitless array of suppositions about things which combine into a definite sense of a matter at hand are suppositions, says Newman, insofar as they offer a *probability* of truth. They are not hypotheses, not working theories in the sense of explicit propositions awaiting some certain demonstration of their veracity. That is, they are 'implicit' and, again, there are far too many of them, and their 'fineness' means many of them are delicately related to the matter at hand, operating more like resonances or suggestive allusions than determined propositions. Nor is Newman using the word 'probability' as it is more commonly used in, say, statistics, where there are explicit, numerical grounds for holding that something is more certain to happen than another. A probability, for Newman, is the basis for giving assent to something in the complexity of daily life, where we simply have to decide for or against something with different form of certainty to that of deductive inference. There is a vast range of such probabilities at work in empirical reasoning, that is, reasoning in life: life embodied and social. By describing these, Newman seeks to capture 'the multiform and intricate process of ratiocination' of the human being 'as a concrete fact'.[8]

The illative sense is the sense we have of a matter at hand in arriving at this informally inferred assent to it. Our illative assents proceed by way of 'the cumulation of probabilities, independent of each other, arising out of the nature and circumstances of the particular case which is under review'.[9] The word 'sense' is used as referring to a general awareness, as the term is used in textual hermeneutics

---

7. Ibid., p. 281.
8. Ibid.
9. Ibid.

as distinguished from the more clearly determined and formal 'meaning'.[10] Indeed, it is helpful to mention the hermeneutical circle here, insofar as it is often presented as an alternative to the reasoning of the natural sciences, which has a grounding basis in explicitly arrived-at conclusions via inductive inference. In reading texts we have a general 'sense' of what the text is about, usually without any clear line of argumentation as to why it has this 'sense'. Similarly, with the illative sense for a matter at hand, we gave 'a mental comprehension of the whole sense, and a discernment of its upshot', which Newman describes as 'an unwritten summing-up'.[11] The illative sense is not always spontaneous, he clarifies, it can often be deliberative. Whether it comes 'after much deliberation' or 'by a clear and rapid act of the intellect', is has contributory, constitutive, and cumulating judgements which combine into it and are made on the basis of probabilities, on instinctively choosing that things do or not pertain. Even when deliberative, moreover, the vast multiplicity of probabilities undergirding each matter at hand are so many that they cannot be broken down into premises, in terms of both volume and complexly varying resonantial intensity or acuteness.

Newman thus defines the illative sense as the 'power of judging about truth and error in concrete matters', as a sort of 'instinctive correctness'.[12] Hermeneutic theorists like Gadamer point to how personal our 'sense' of a text is, how it is naturally relative to our standpoint and suppositions and prejudices.[13] The same is true of course for the illative sense. With it, we have a sense for the matter at hand in which we 'judge for ourselves, by our own lights, and on our own principles' and thus 'our criterion of truth is not so much the manipulation of propositions, as the intellectual and moral character of the person maintaining them'.[14] This helps explain certain statements Newman makes in the *Apologia* about his own struggles with truth and error. He says he had always had 'a great dislike of paper logic', and that 'it was not logic that carried me on'. Were the horse put before the cart, we read, it would be like saying 'that the quicksilver in the barometer changes the weather'. No, 'it is the concrete being that reasons', for 'the whole man moves; paper logic is but the record of it'.[15] Put into context with statements like these, we can understand why Mary Katherine Tillman writes that Newman's 'relatively brief discussion of the illative sense' in the *Grammar* 'is disproportionate to its tacit preponderance in all of his writings'.[16]

---

10. See Wilhelm Dilthey, *Selected Works Volume 3: The Formation of the Historical World in the Human Sciences*, edited by Rudolf A. Makkreel and Frithjof Rodi (Princeton, NJ: Princeton University Press, 2002), pp. 254–5.

11. Newman, *Grammar*, pp. 284–5.

12. Ibid., p. 346.

13. See Carr, *Newman and Gadamer*.

14. Newman, *Grammar*, p. 295.

15. Ibid., p. 218.

16. Mary Katherine Tillman, *John Henry Newman: Man of Letters* (Milwaukee: Marquette University Press, 2015), p. 216.

The empiricism of the illative sense is already self-evident from the foregoing, but Newman extenuates it by arguing that the illative sense is structurally analogous to sensory perception. He writes, 'an object of sense presents itself to our view as a whole ... we take it in, recognise it, and discriminate it from other options'. Yet this is all unreflective, it simply carries on, moment by moment, in concrete life, just like the illative sense.[17] The deep empiricism on display here is further indicated by the fact Newman enters into an extended discussion with British empiricist philosophy, particularly with John Locke, David Hume, and Francis Bacon. But, while Cameron argues that Newman is so proximate to this school that he is a mere theological counterpart to British empiricism, and Jay Newman agrees that he 'works largely within the framework of traditional British empiricism',[18] the actual substance of his argument rather challenges the entire tradition of this philosophical school for not being empirical enough. Hence, Fey is correct to say that he is 'not Lockean in intention', and that 'the whole tenor and purpose of Newman's work was to challenge Locke's presuppositions' and make them more empirical. Fey rightly concludes that 'Newman's position cannot fairly be treated as Cameron has suggested'.[19]

To return to the point at issue: the profoundly empirical orientation of the *Grammar* irons out the tension between the *Development* essay and the condemnation of the English as antithetical to history from the *Present Position*. *Development*'s empiricism is, as with the *Grammar*'s, an empiricism of the living embodied present, of empirical consciousness, and is therefore in a way more empirical than even the British empiricists. Importantly, moreover, Newman's discussion of the illative sense enables him finally to reach a point where the empiricism of the English sensibility is praised, and not condemned. Moreover, it is praised in and of itself, not in relation to grace or the supernatural. We have seen Newman focusing on 'ratiocination as the exercise of the living faculty in the individual intellect' as sharply distinguished from 'mere skill in argumentative science'. He then claims this distinction is 'the true interpretation of the prejudice which exists against logic' in the English 'popular mind'. That is, the old trope that 'Englishmen are too practical to be logical, [and] that an ounce of common-sense goes further than many cartloads of logic'.[20] This juncture is where, at last, we glimpse that there is something intrinsic to the English sensibility which makes it importantly prefigured as appropriate to the Catholic faith. The illative sense is applied to the epistemics of religious belief and not just assent per se; it is Newman's empiricism which enables him to challenge rationalist critiques of Christian faith.

Here we can detect a continuity between Englishness and Catholicism which is not present during the period of the Second Spring. Immediately post-conversion,

---

17. Newman, *Grammar*, p. 294.
18. Jay Newman, *Mental Philosophy*, p. 74.
19. William R. Fey, *Faith and Doubt: The Unfolding of Newman's Thought on Certainty* (Shepherdstown, WV: Patmos Press, 1976), pp. 21–2, 77, 82.
20. Newman, *Grammar*, pp. 295–6.

Newman held that England's becoming Catholic must be a countercultural move, a sheer 'miracle' going entirely against the grain of all that went before. Now he has arrived at something which makes a particular aspect of Englishness highly serviceable for Catholic truth.

11.2 Pragmatic development and empirical consciousness

The illative sense enables us to see Newman rediscovering and integrating English empiricism into his mature thought, in terms of the epistemics of belief, at least. There remains a tension with empiricism, however, rooted in the Tractarian period, where Newman deviates from the traditional principles of pragmatism in his writing on the *via media*. This tension is intensified significantly during the Second Spring period, where pragmatism's concomitants – industrialization and the parliamentary tradition – are presented as grounded on errant 'assumed principles' at the core of English identity.

Now, attentive readers will have discerned that the *Development* essay evinces an empirical pragmatism of sorts, and thus stands within a broadly Burkean orientation as regards the organic development of the Church. However, the Church as Newman understands it in that work, bequeathed by Christ to the Apostles, is obviously not seen as errant at root like the Church of England as bequeathed by Henry VIII to his courtiers. In terms of collective, social development, one cannot deny or downplay Newman's view of the Reformation as a fundamental breach cutting through the heart of Christianity itself. That is, Anglicanism cannot develop into Catholicism through a patient accumulation of modifications and corrections cumulatively contributing to a better common sense of the things of God. Any continuity here is impossible to envisage.

However, the *Apologia*, as autobiographical, does indeed chart Newman's development *from* Anglicanism into Catholicism, and the irruption of grace into an individual life must always make use of the circumstances it gracefully encounters, modifying and correcting them over time. Newman therefore describes his aims for the *Apologia* as being to describe his 'living intelligence', to give the 'true key to my whole life'.[21] He says, 'I will draw out' the 'history of my mind', stating 'the point at which I began, in what external suggestion or accident each opinion had its rise, how far and how they developed from within, how they grew, were modified, were combined, were in collision with each other, and were changed'.[22] In this process, the 'probability' later discussed at length in the *Grammar* is described as 'the guide of life', and Newman thereby charts, point by point, his developing towards the final assent to the Church of Rome that materialized in 1845.[23]

---

21. Newman, *Apologia*, p. 83.
22. Ibid., p. 84.
23. Ibid., pp. 94 and 100.

The point is that, viewed autobiographically, from the perspective of individual experience, Newman is able to show how his natural state as un-Catholic fed into and was eventually perfected by the supernatural grace he received from the Catholic Church. Hence Turner's comment about Newman's Catholicism 'emerging from a Protestant chrysalis'.[24] It is this shift to the individual perspective which enables him to make those more conciliatory statements about Anglicanism discussed in Chapter 9. Viewed from this perspective, conversion is not just a volte-face; one can claim there is 'a blessing through obedience even to an erroneous system' and 'guidance even by means of it out of it'.[25] Elements of Anglicanism, of Englishness as he knew it, did in this sense lead him to Rome. This is because those elements are true, like the suspicion of paper logic, and truth has 'a power of self-correcting virtue and a power of germinating'.[26] The possibility that Englishness can, as perfected by grace, germinate into the flowering of Catholic life is something Newman arrives at by virtue of his stanchly empirical method, in this case autobiography, and it also applies to empiricism itself. For Newman, Catholicism is an empirical religion. As Ian Ker writes, it was the 'external objective reality' of the Catholic faith that most impressed him after his conversion, particularly regarding the reservation of the Blessed Sacrament.[27] The material presence of Christ as given to the living empirical present was a 'central aspect of the impact of Catholicism on the imagination' of the English Protestant convert. In short, this was where his heart was tending as an Anglican, and where it led him as a Catholic.[28]

As it stands, it might seem we need to leave the mature Newman's continuity with empirical pragmatism as something that can be applied only to an individual life-trajectory, not the breaches of social and civic life. Yet another of Newman's conciliatory passages from the *Apologia* provides an example to understand how we might consider Englishness undergoing graced perfection in a much broader sense. Here, he argues that 'the multitude of nations which are within the fold of the Church' have 'acted for its protection, against any narrowness' on the part of Rome. He goes on, 'national influences have a providence effect in moderation the bias which the local influences of Italy may exert upon the See of St Peter'. Moreover, 'the loss of the English, not to say the German element' has been a grave 'misfortune' to the Church. He then turns to Pius IX's restoration of the hierarchy. But, unlike the Second Spring sermon this restoration is not presented only as a radical breach or irruption with what went before. Rather, Newman can now claim the pope 'has prepared a way for our own habits of mind, our own manner of reasoning, our own tastes, and our own virtues', to find 'a place and thereby a sanctification, in the Catholic Church'.[29]

24. Turner, *Evangelical Religion*, p. 294.
25. Ibid., p. 247.
26. Ibid.
27. Ker, *Catholic Revival*, p. 31.
28. Ibid., p. 19.
29. Newman, *Apologia*, p. 296.

11.3 Summary

The foregoing discussion would suggest that, when it comes to Newman's empiricism, his mature writings do indeed integrate his earliest empirical commitments. The method of the *Grammar* and the deeply empirical illative sense enable us to see how his method in *Development* is not recanted by his dismissals of the English 'antipathy to fact' in the *Present Position*. The same discussion enables us to see how there is an aspect to English empiricism which he stands by to the end, the dislike of 'paper logic' compared to the objective, present reality. Moreover, Newman's writing out of the course of his own intellectual and spiritual development in the *Apologia* entails that he discerns aspects of 'nature', the circumstances of his life, which do feed into his supernatural life as a Catholic. Again, this eventually enables him to stand fast to English 'habits of mind', 'manners of reasoning', 'tastes', and 'virtues' as relatively good in and of themselves and thus able to find 'a place and thereby a sanctification' in the Catholic Church.

When it comes to English empiricism, the emphasis of the nature–grace relation is significantly different to both compromise and reserve. With compromise, it is grace working against nature and contradicting it. With reserve, there is a way back to nature 'after' all is undone by God's grace in conversion. With empiricism, however, nature actively feeds into the life of grace, guiding it towards God and finding a 'place and a sanctification' in the divine life thereafter. Newman's empiricism is eventually shown to be a hugely significant aspect to his Catholic theology, and something from which he never departs. As with reserve, interestingly, this empiricism far extends beyond the range of something exclusively English, although Newman's Englishness grounds his affection for it. Catholicism itself has English aspects, not least in the objective, material reality of the Blessed Sacrament.

Chapter 12

CONCLUSION: DISTANT SCENE

Commentators frequently mention either Newman's Englishness or his un-Englishness, yet Englishness itself has not been analysed in detail in the scholarship on Newman's theology. I can now conclude that those commentators who draw attention to Newman as English or un-English are, in a certain sense, both correct, at least as regards his theology. The foregoing chapters enable us to see where Newman is markedly English: in his praising of the instinct for compromise of the Tractarian *via media*, and his wholehearted adoption of an affection for reserve in *Arians*, not to mention the prioritizing of action over idea in the *Parochial and Plain Sermons*. At the same time, however, even the Tractarian Newman strains against his own English sensibility. This is shown particularly with his attempts to determine the ground of the *via media* to such a degree that it undermines it as a compromise settlement, and how this same intention breaks with notions of Burkean development as empirical pragmatism.

Newman's Tractarian un-Englishness is dramatically intensified in the Second Spring period, where the *via media* is entirely forsaken and Newman radically departs from his prior affection for compromise in *Difficulties* and the *Development* essay. Similarly, reserve is explicitly critiqued with his discovery of the supernatural virtue of faith in *Difficulties*. When it comes to empiricism, while *Development* is unique among his writings from this period in evincing an empirical method, in the *Present Position* Newman implies that even this method should be considered un-English, because the English are antithetical to historical fact.

Were we to leave the discussion here, it would seem that Newman develops from an awkward relationship with the English sensibility into becoming a full-blown foreigner in his own land. However, we have seen that the mature Newman actually integrates his Englishness with his Catholicism, but he does so in a way that does not negate or undermine the drama and significance of his post-conversion period. That is, compromise remains forsaken, and on this front Newman is enduringly un-English. Reserve does reappear through the possibility of cultivated affections proceeding on the basis of the supernatural virtue of faith – presenting the possibility of there being such a thing as a Catholic, English gentleman. Empiricism proves particularly important, for here Newman praises the empirical mindset of the English sensibility and we can include this, then, as belonging to 'our own habits of mind' which find 'a place and thereby a sanctification, in the Catholic Church'.

Newman is thus not only both English and un-English in different ways at different times, he is enduringly English and enduringly un-English in his mature work. The elements at play can therefore now be applied to the discussion of the Power of Assimilation with which this book began. There, Newman describes how Christianity develops through a lively encounter with the world around it, through which 'materials appropriated come to belong to it and enter into its unity'. Firstly, some materials it encounters are discarded, like much pertaining to 'the paganism of old', and are thus destroyed in being 'subjected to a new sovereign'. Secondly, other materials, coming under the influence of this same sovereign, can be 'purified' and 'transmuted' and thus become a 'new element of order and composition' for the faith. Thirdly, some materials can readily be absorbed, because there is 'an antecedent affinity' between them and the truth of Christianity.[1]

Applying this to the foregoing discussion, then, the English instinct for compromise – at least as applied to matters of faith – cannot endure when coming under the new sovereign, Christ. For Newman, the truth of the Gospel must ever dictate that 'holiness before peace'.[2] The English affection for reserve, however, can be purified and transmuted. Reserve can be cleansed of the Pelagian tendencies arising from mistaking decorum and good manners for the things of God and never allowed to undermine intrinsic aspects of the faith, like credal doxology. Finally, English empiricism is shown to be an aspect of Englishness which evinces an antecedent affinity with the faith itself. Here, there is something belonging to the received notion of Englishness which stands in a particularly proximate relationship to the Catholic faith.

During the Second Spring period, I began to apply the language of nature and supernature, or grace, to the relationship between Englishness and Catholicism. In the ways Newman forsakes or integrates aspects of his Englishness in the mature period, this nomenclature proved helpful for classifying the different interrelationships at play, which each align roughly with differing emphases of this relationship. Compromise shows a moment where grace entirely undoes nature, a moment of radical rebirth. Reserve shows how nature is sometimes graciously elevated, asymmetrically, after all has been surrendered to grace. Empiricism shows how nature itself can lead to grace and then be perfected by it; indeed, we glimpse here something like what Tillman connects with Newman's 'unity of type' when it blends with a particular: a 'concrete universal'.[3]

We therefore end with a sense of what it might mean to think more broadly about Newman's struggles with the English sensibility. Insofar as reserve proves capable of a graced reconfiguration after irruption, and empiricism tends towards

---

1. Newman, *Development*, p. 187.
2. A motto by Thomas Scott oft-repeated by Newman, see Thomas J. Norris, 'Faith', in *The Cambridge Companion to John Henry Newman*, pp. 73–97, 76.
3. Tillman, *Man of Letters*, pp. 258–9.

a graced perfection only God can bring, we see something like elements of cultural particularity reaching universal provenance. That is, we have theological substance to apply to the contention that Newman 'belongs to every time and place and people', and how 'his insights ... were not only of profound importance for Victorian England' but should 'continue today to inspire and enlighten many all over the world'.[4] Perhaps here we glimpse something of an authentically English Catholicism. To be such, it must be no less authentically Catholic than it is authentically English, and it must evince both proximity and distance from its native setting, for 'the death of God ... submerges all culture'.[5] As such, however, it bespeaks a mindset of careful reserve towards knowledge and words about God, arising from a marked concern for the living, embodied present as the site of God's transformative action in the many twists and turns of human life:

> I do not wish to see
> The distant scene
> One step enough for me

---

4. John Paul II and Benedict XVI, quoted by Tillman, *Man of Letters*, 16 nn. 4 and 6.
5. Robert Cardinal Sarah, *The Power of Silence: Against the Dictatorship of Noise* (San Francisco, CA: Ignatius Press, 2017), p. 140.

BIBLIOGRAPHY

Works by Newman

An Essay in Aid of a Grammar of Assent, London: Burns, Oates, 1870.
An Essay on the Development of Christian Doctrine, edited by James Cameron, Middlesex: Pelican Books, 1974.
An Essay on the Development of Christian Doctrine, edited by Ian Ker, Indiana: University of Notre Dame Press, 1989.
Apologia pro vita sua, London: J. M. Dent, 1993.
Arians of the fourth century, their doctrine, temper, and conduct, chiefly as exhibited in the Councils of the Church, between A.D. 325, & A.D. 381, London: E. Lumley, 1871.
Arians of the Fourth Century, Leominster: Gracewing, 2001.
Certain Difficulties Felt by of Anglicans in Catholic Teaching Volume 1, New York: Longmans, Green, 1901.
Characteristics from the writings of John Henry Newman, edited by William Samuel Lilly, New York: Scribner, Welford, & Armstrong, 1875.
Discourses to Mixed Congregations, London: Longmans, Green, 1906.
Discussions and Arguments, New York: Longmans, Green, 1907.
'Elliot's Travels', *British Critic*, vol. 25 (April 1839), 305–20
Faith and Prejudice and Other Sermons, New York: Sheed & Ward, 1956.
The Idea of a University, Yale: Yale University Press, 1996.
Lectures on Justification, London: Longmans, Green, 1892.
Lectures on the Present Position of Catholics in England, Leominster: Gracewing, 2000.
Lectures on the Prophetical Office of the Church: Via Media Volume 1, London: Longmans, Green, 1901.
A Letter Addressed to the Duke of Norfolk on Occasion of Mr. Gladstone's Recent Expostulation: Certain Difficulties Felt by Anglicans in Catholic Teaching Volume 2, New York: Longmans, Green, 1900.
The Letters and Diaries of John Henry Cardinal Newman: Vol. I: Ealing, Trinity, Oriel, February 1801 to December 1826, edited by I. Ker and T. Gornall, Oxford: Clarendon Press, 1979.
The Letters and Diaries of John Henry Newman: Volume II: Tutor of Oriel, January 1827 to December 1831, edited by I. Ker and T. Gornall, Oxford: Clarendon Press, 1979.
The Letters and Diaries of John Henry Newman: Volume III: New Bearings: January 1832 to June 1833, edited by I. Ker and T. Gornall, Oxford: Clarendon Press, 1979.
Loss & Gain, Leominster: Gracewing, 2014.
'Palmer's Treatise on the Church of Christ', *British Critic*, vol. 24 (October 1838), 179–215.
Parochial and Plain Sermons, San Francisco, CA: Ignatius Press, 1997.
Sermons Preached on Various Occasions, London: Longmans, Green, 1908.

[Newman and other] Members of the University of Oxford, *Tracts for the Times Volume One; 1833–1834 Tracts 1–46 and Records of the Church 1–18*, edited by Christopher Poore, Galesburg, IL: Seminary Street Press, 2021.

Other works

Ackroyd, Peter, *Albion: The Origins of the English Imagination*, London: Vintage Press, 2004.
Arnold, Matthew, *Culture and Anarchy*, New Haven, CT: Yale University Press, 1994.
Arnold, Matthew, *Essays in Criticism: Second Series*, London: Macmillan, 1935.
Bromwich, David, *The Intellectual Life of Edmund Burke: From the Sublime and Beautiful to American Independence*, Cambridge, MA: Belknap Press of Harvard University Press, 2014.
Brown, Stuart (ed.), *Routledge History of Philosophy Volume V: British Empiricism and the Enlightenment*, London: Taylor & Francis, 2003.
Burke, Edmund, *The Portable Burke*, edited by Isaac Kramnik, Harmondsworth: Penguin, 1999.
Burke, Edmund, *Reflections on the Revolutions in France*, Oxford: Oxford University Press, 1950.
Cameron, J. M., *John Henry Newman*, London: Longmans, Green, 1956.
Carr, Thomas K., *Newman and Gadamer: Toward a Hermeneutics of Religious Knowledge*, Oxford: Oxford University Press, 1996.
Collini, Stefan, *English Pasts: Essays in History and Culture*, Oxford: Oxford University Press, 1999.
Connolly, John R., *John Henry Newman: A View of Catholic Faith for the New Millennium*, Lanham, MD: Rowland and Littlefield, 2005.
Cornwell, John, *Newman's Unquiet Grave: The Reluctant Saint*, London: Continuum, 2010.
Coulsen, John, *Newman and the Common Tradition: A Study in the Language of Church and Society*, Oxford: Oxford University Press, 1970.
Coverley, Merlin, *Psychogeography*, Hertfordshire: Oldcastle Books, 2006.
Cross, F. L., and E. A. Livingstone, *The Oxford Dictionary of the Christian Church*, 3rd edn, Oxford: Oxford University Press, 2005.
Curran, Stuart (ed.), *The Cambridge Companion to British Romanticism*, Cambridge: Cambridge University Press, 1993.
D'Curz, K. S. G., F. A., *Cardinal Newman: His Place in Religion and Literature*, Madras: Good Pastor Press, 1935.
Dilthey, Wilhelm, *Selected Works Volume 3: The Formation of the Historical World in the Human Sciences*, edited by Rudolf A. Makkreel and Frithjof Rodi, Princeton, NJ: Princeton University Press, 2002.
Doyle, Brian, *English and Englishness*, London: Taylor & Francis, 2013.
Dulles S. J., Avery, 'Newman on Infallibility', *Theological Studies*, vol. 51 (1990), 434–49.
Eagleton, Terry, *Culture*, Yale: Yale University Press, 2018.
Eagleton, Terry, *Literary Theory; An Introduction*, 2nd edn, Oxford: Blackwell, 1996.
Easthope, Anthony, *Englishness and National Culture*, London: Routledge, 1999.
Fey, William R., *Faith and Doubt: The Unfolding of Newman's Thought on Certainty*, Shepherdstown, WV: Patmos Press, 1976.

Goslee, David, *Romanticism and the Anglican Newman*, Athens: Ohio University Press, 1996.
Guarino, Thomas G., *Vincent of Lérins and the Development of Christian Doctrine*, Grand Rapids, MI: Baker Academic, 2013.
Hastings, Adrian (ed.), *The Oxford Companion to Christian Thought*, Oxford: Oxford University Press, 2000.
Herbert, George, *The Poems of George Herbert*, Oxford: Oxford University Press, 1961.
Holtzen, T., 'The Anglican Via Media: The Idea of Moderation in Reform', *Journal of Anglican Studies*, vol. 17, no. 1 (2019): 48-73.
Hopkins, Gerald Manley, *Further Letters of Gerard Manley Hopkins including His Correspondence with Coventry Patmore*, edited by Claude Colleer Abbott, Oxford: Oxford University Press, 1938.
Jost, Walter, *Rhetorical Thought in John Henry Newman*, South Carolina: University of South Carolina Press, 1989.
Ker, Ian, *John Henry Newman: A Biography*, Oxford: Oxford University Press, 2010.
Ker, Ian, *Newman on Being a Christian*, South Bend: Notre Dame University Press, 1990.
Ker, Ian, *The Catholic Revival in English Literature 1845-1961*, Leominster: Gracewing, 2003.
Ker, Ian, and Terrence Merrigan, *The Cambridge Companion to John Henry Newman*, Cambridge: Cambridge University Press, 2009.
Langford, Paul, *Englishness Identified: Manners and Character 1650-1850*, Oxford: Oxford University Press, 2001.
Langham, Mark, *The Caroline Divines and the Church of Rome: A Contribution to Current Ecumenical Dialogue*, London: Routledge, 2018.
Luther, Martin, *Luther's German Bible of 1522*, translated by Robert E. Smith from *Dr. Martin Luther's Vermischte Deutsche Schriften Volume 63*, Erlangen: Heyder and Zimmer, 1854.
Meszaros, Andrew, *The Prophetic Church: History and Doctrinal Development in John Henry Newman and Yves Congar*, Oxford: Oxford University Press, 2016.
Morrow, John, *Thomas Carlyle*, London: Continuum, 2006.
Nabe, Clyde, *Mystery and Religion: Newman's Epistemology of Religion*, Lanham, MD: University Press of America, 1988.
Newman, Jay, *The Mental Philosophy of John Henry Newman*, Ontario: Wilfred Laurier University Press, 1986.
O'Brien, Conor Cruise, *The Great Melody*, London: Sinclair Stevenson, 1992.
Owen, H. P., *The Moral Argument for Christian Theism*, London: Allen & Unwin, 1965.
Pevsner, Nikolaus, *The Englishness of English Art*, London: Penguin Books, 1964.
Phillips, Jacob, 'Raymond Williams' Reading of Newman's The Idea of a University' *New Blackfriars*, vol. 102. 10.1111/nbfr.12564.
Phillips, Jacob, 'John Henry Newman and the English Sensibility', *Logos; A Journal of Catholic Thought and Culture*, vol. 24, no. 3 (2021): 108-29.
Rowland, Tracey (ed.), *The Anglican Patrimony in Catholic Communion: The Gift of the Ordinariates*, London: T&T Clark, 2021.
Ruskin, John, *The Complete Works of John Ruskin Volume XXXIII*, edited by E. T. Cook and A. Wedderburn, London: George Allen & Unwin, 1903-12.
Scruton, Roger, *England: An Elegy*, London: Continuum, 2006.
Short, Edward, *Newman and His Contemporaries*, London: T&T Clark Continuum, 2015.
Thompson, E. P., 'The Peculiarities of the English', *Socialist Register*, vol. 2 (1965), 311-62.

Tillman, Mary Katherine, *John Henry Newman: Man of Letters*, Milwaukee: Marquette University Press, 2015.
Turner, Frank M., *John Henry Newman: The Challenge to Evangelical Religion*, Yale: Yale University Press, 2002.
Viviano, Benedict Thomas, *Catholic Hermeneutics Today: Critical Essays*, Eugene, OR: Wipf and Stock, 2014.
Walgrave, J. H., *Newman the Theologian: The Nature of Belief and Doctrine as Exemplified in His Life and Works*, New York: Sheed & Ward, 1960.
Weatherby, Harold L., *Cardinal Newman in His Age*, Vanderbilt: Vanderbilt University Press, 1973.
Williams, Raymond, *Culture and Society 1780–1950*, Harmondsworth: Penguin Books, 1963.
Winder, Robert, *The Last Wolf: The Hidden Springs of Englishness*, London: Little Brown Group, 2017.
Yanitelli, Victor R., *A Newman Symposium*, New York: Fordham University Press, 1952.
Young, Arthur, *The Example of France a Warning to Britain*, Dublin, 1793.

INDEX

Ackroyd, Peter 21–4
Addison, Joseph 15
Aquinas 77
Aristotle 64, 97
Arnold, Matthew 24, 26–8
St Athanasius 45, 63–4

Bacon, Francis 27, 125
Browne, Thomas 27
Burke, Edmund 14–16, 24, 28, 58–9, 75, 96, 111

Cameron, James M. 28, 60, 83, 105, 116, 125
Caroline Divines 31, 41, 44, 53, 56
Chadwick, Owen 105
Chaucer, Geoffrey 26
Collini, Stefan 18, 25, 27
Cooper, Anthony Ashley 15
Cornwell, John 3
Coulson, John 3, 101
culture 5, 15–16

disciplina arcani 43–4, 46
D'Curz K.S.G., F. A. 3
Donne, John 60
Doyle, Brian 19
Dulles, Avery 105

Eagleton, Terry 14–15
Easthope, Anthony 14
Edward Bouverie Pusey 58, 78, 116
Elliot, Charles Boileau 22

faith (supernatural virtue) 74–8
Fremantle, Anne 3
Froude, Hurrell 25, 76
Froude, James Anthony 94
Fuseli, Henry 27

Gaurino, Thomas G. 2
Gladstone, William 106
Gorham, George 88
Gower, John 26

Herbert, George 25–6
Honan, Daniel J. 3
Hooker, Richard 31, 41, 45, 56, 60
Hume, David 125

illative sense 123–5

Keble, Thomas 33
Ker, Ian 2, 8, 15, 71, 83, 105, 127
Kingsley, Charles 6, 10, 94–102, 110

Langford, Paul 13, 18, 20, 26–7
Langham, Mark 31
Liouri, Alphonsus 78
Locke, John 125
Lord Morley 3
Luther, Martin 77

McCarren, Gerard H. 2
Manning, Henry Edward 3
Marian devotion 78–81
Merrigan, Terrence 2
Möhler, Johann Adam 8, 17
Monophysite controversy 64
mystery 57, 93, 102–4

Newman, John Henry
   An Essay in Aid of a Grammar of Assent 5, 17, 102–6, 111–19, 121–8
   An Essay on the Development of Christian Doctrine 1–2, 8–10, 65, 69, 73–4, 79, 83–6, 90, 98, 109, 121, 124, 126, 128–9

Apologia pro vita sua 9–11, 61, 63, 76, 93–102, 110–11, 116, 124, 126–7
Arians of the Fourth Century 3, 7, 9, 42–51, 53–5, 73, 76, 79–80, 104, 109, 117
Certain Difficulties Felt by Anglicans in Catholic Teaching 8, 11, 22, 63–4, 66, 71, 75–80, 87–90, 95–6, 99, 106, 109, 115, 129
Idea of a University 10, 72, 78–9, 86
Lectures on Justification 57
Lectures on the Present Position of Catholics in England 6, 10, 22–3, 68, 85–6, 88, 90, 104–5, 121, 124, 128
Letter to the Duke of Norfolk 105
Loss and Gain 6, 16, 65, 67–9, 72, 89, 101
Parochial and Plain Sermons 5, 7, 54–7, 60, 83, 91, 121, 129
The Prophetical Office of the Church 6, 33–40, 59–60, 64, 67, 69, 71, 83, 93, 98–100

Oxford Movement 6

Palmer, William 34, 39, 70
papal infallibility 104–6
Percival, Philip 33
Pevsner, Nicolaus 21, 26, 29
Philpotts, Henry 88
Pius IX 127
Power of Assimilation 1, 66, 130

Queen Victoria 2

Rose, Hugh 3

Sarolea, Charles 3
Scruton, Roger 21
Shakespeare, William 25
Short, Edward 4
Simpson, David 17, 23
Steele, Richard 15

Taylor, William (of Norwich) 13
Thomas, Stephen 44, 105
Thompson, E. 27
Thorndike, Herbert 41
Tillman, Mary Katherine 124, 130
Tracts for the Times 7, 12, 32, 34, 43, 57, 93
Turner, Frank 3, 9, 100, 127

via media 5–6, 9, 31–6, 38–41, 57–8, 60, 63–72, 83, 93–4, 105–6, 121, 126, 129
Viviano, Benedict Thomas 2

Walgrave OP, J. H. 3, 11
Warburton, William 66
Weatherby, Harold L. 11, 56
Winder, Robert 6, 21
William of Malmesbury 25
William of Ockham 27
Williams, Isaac 5, 44
Williams, Raymond 5, 15, 24
Williams, Rowan 44

Young, Arthur 26

www.ingramcontent.com/pod-product-compliance
Lightning Source LLC
Chambersburg PA
CBHW061844300426
44115CB00013B/2496